Wonders of Nuclear Fusion

Wonders of
Nuclear Fusion

Creating an Ultimate Energy Source

Neal Singer

University of New Mexico Press | Albuquerque

Barbara Guth Worlds of Wonder

Science Series for Young Readers

Advisory Editors: David Holtby and Karen Taschek

Please see page 114 for more information about the series.

© 2011 by the University of New Mexico Press
All rights reserved. Published 2011
Printed in China by Four Colour Print Group
Production location: Guangdong, China | Date of Production: 2/7/2011 | Cohort: Batch I
16 15 14 13 12 11   1 2 3 4 5 6

Library of Congress Cataloging-in-Publication Data
Singer, Neal, 1941–
Wonders of nuclear fusion : creating an ultimate energy source / Neal Singer.
p. cm. — (Worlds of wonder)
Includes index.
ISBN 978-0-8263-4778-7 (cloth : alk. paper)
1. Nuclear fusion—Juvenile literature. I. Title.
QC791.5.S56 2011
621.48′4—dc22
2010039325

With special thanks to the University of New Mexico Center for Regional Studies.
Many conceptual drawings provided by Xuan Chen.

Cover: [Z-machine] Arcs and Sparks, the picture of Sandia National Laboratories' Z Machine firing, has been published around the world. The jagged, lightning-like arcings are loved by graphic artists. But they are viewed as failures by engineers. If you look closely, you'll see each electrical arc begins where a piece of metal emerges from the water. The arcs are short circuits—energies that didn't get to their target at the center of the machine. So there's room for improvement, though Z ranks high among fusion machines in efficiency. Sandia photographer Randy Montoya aimed the camera, set it with an open shutter, and left the area before Z fired. (Courtesy Sandia National Laboratories; photographer Randy Montoya)

To my wife, my kids, and the memory of my dad

Contents

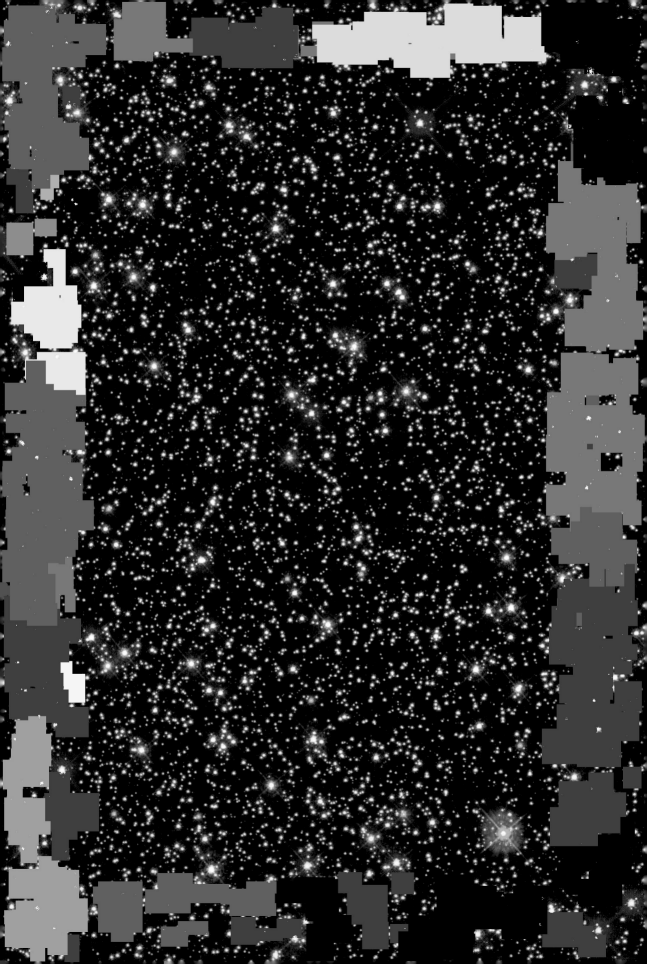

Acknowledgments

Any book requires input from many people. Particularly helpful was the support of editors David Holtby and Karen Taschek; the proof-reading for scientific accuracy by retired Sandia National Laboratories physicist Tom Sanford and by Phil Schewe, author, physicist, and senior science writer at the American Institute of Physics; Bob Hirschfeld, hardworking public information officer at Lawrence Livermore National Laboratory; the drawings of artist Xuan Chen; the photo coordination of Felicia Cedillos; the copyediting of Ginny Hoffman; and the line-by-line editing of certain book chapters by my daughter Sarany Singer and student Laura Montoya.

First impressions are hard to change: Early nuclear bomb tests provided beautiful but terrifying images of the new atomic science. (Picture courtesy of National Nuclear Security Administration Nevada Site Office)

CHAPTER 1
Cosmic Blending

Fusion is something that happens with music, where different styles are harmonized to create a new blend. And there are fusion styles in food, too—Asian and Mexican are blended to make new tastes, for example. But what we're discussing here isn't the chemical joining of *atoms* or intermingling of sound wavelengths, but something . . . new. Something . . . dangerous. Something so powerful it was first tested as a terribly destructive weapon, the hydrogen bomb.

This is *nuclear fusion*—fusion of the *nuclei* of atoms. But nuclear fusion doesn't have to be a weapon. The governments of earth are spending billions of dollars to harness the process for peaceful purposes. Because if they do, if it can be done, there'll never be another war over energy. One bathtub half-filled with seawater, for example, would yield the electrical energy of 40 train cars of coal.

So everyone wants nuclear fusion. And governments think they can get it. But the main question is: what is the best way to control it?

And first of all: what is it?

A hundred years ago, people looked up at the sun and wondered, what could be burning like that? Coal, some people figured. They knew that wood burned with uplifted flames, and coal burned with quiet intensity, and the sun didn't look like a wood fire. So, then, coal. The sun is a big lump of burning coal that, like any fire, gave off light and heat. But the data didn't match. I mean, gentle reader,

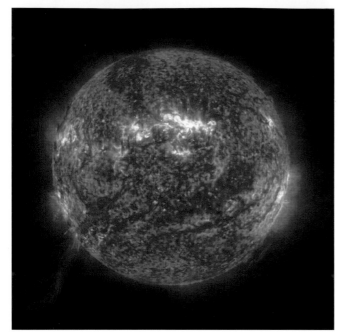

Earth's energy source: Far more powerful than any bomb created by humans, the sun is powered by the energy released by huge numbers of atoms fusing. (Courtesy NASA)

how would you compute it? Our forebears were reasonable. First, they figured—from the size of the sun and the amount of heat it gave off—how long it would last before it burned down to a cinder. A big piece of coal giving off light and heat. Hmmm . . . it would last only a few thousand years. Not a long time. That theory seemed odd. Especially since no one had noticed the sun getting smaller year by year. Well, how long had it been burning? The sun couldn't have been much bigger than it was now because a really huge sun in the sky wouldn't have looked like any of the ancient pictures made thousands of years ago by the early Egyptians and Greeks. The best birth age that calculations could come up with, without making the sun Godzilla huge, was a few thousand years ago.

But everyone agreed, even people who literally interpreted the Bible, that the earth was older than a few thousand years. That just brought us back to the time of the Romans and Jesus. It didn't get us back to Moses, three thousand years ago, Abraham, four thousand years ago, or, to anthropologists, cave paintings thirty thousand years ago. Then there are paleogeologists—people who study the earth and its creatures as they may have existed long, long ago—who believe that a massive die-off killed 95 percent of all life on earth 251 million years ago. (If true, we're all evolved from that remaining 5 percent—creatures who burrowed in the earth and didn't need much oxygen. Look how much freer we've become!) I could go on, but you get the point: no way a lump of coal had burned all that time.

So theorists were stuck. How could the sun last for billions of years before us (as scientists currently believe) and presumably for billions of years after us? And send out so much heat and light? What's the trick, doc? How does the sun do it? Inquiring minds want to know.

For thousands and thousands of years, the human race had no idea. The sun went up, it went across, it went down. It was only 100 years ago, a very small part of human history, that a young man figured out the basics of it. He was about the age of a lot of rock stars of today; his name was Albert Einstein. Usually you see pictures of him as an old man with wild hair and sad eyes wearing a sweatshirt, and he looks kind of cool for an old guy. But when he did this work, he was a young man in his early twenties.

He couldn't get a job at a university. Just couldn't compete with the people who got As in class and didn't argue with the professors. Also, Einstein was Jewish and faced discrimination. He managed to support himself and his little family with a job in a patent office in Switzerland. Every day, the person we now consider the smartest person of the 20th century went to work, examining ideas from people who wanted to patent anything from potato peelers to impossible perpetual motion machines. At night, he went home to his small apartment, which was above a store in the shopping district of downtown Berne. He didn't have access to laboratories and equipment. So he ate dinner with his wife, sat on his old couch, and at a small desk in his little apartment, from his mind he derived a formula that is the most famous formula in physics. It's called $E = mc^2$. Have you heard of it?

It's a pretty simple formula to be so famous. But it's okay to be simple in science. The formula says that if you could convert *mass* (*m*)—that's this book, or a pencil or a cat or a tree or an apple and so on—directly into *energy* (*E*), that energy would equal the converted mass of the object times the speed of light (*c*) squared.

Transmission lines bring electricity from generating plants into communities, where it powers our many plug-in appliances.

What is mass? Consider your body. A scale would say you weigh a certain amount. But away from Earth's gravity—on a spaceship between planets, say—you would weigh almost nothing. Yet you would still have the same body. So weight varies, depending on gravity.

Mass doesn't vary. Mass represents the amount of material something is made of. For us, on Earth, weight and mass come to pretty much the same thing. It's true your weight is slightly less on top of a tall mountain, where gravity is less (you're farther from the mass at the center of the Earth) than it would be at sea level. But Einstein meant his equation to work anywhere, on Earth or in space, so he used the term *mass*.

Now, the speed of light is a big number: 186,000 miles per second (150,000 kilometers per second). My calculator tells me that number multiplied by itself (squared) equals 34,596,000,000. So if you could turn a crumb of bread completely into energy, according to Einstein, you would multiply its tiny mass by that very big number. That crumb would give us a lot of energy. Ten million times more energy, on a weight-by-weight basis, than many more ordinary chemical reactions—like burning gasoline—that surround us every day.

We want that kind of energy. *Nuclear fusion* energy.

Of course, it will be a long time before we can use just any piece of matter—bread, oranges, whatever—for nuclear fusion fuel. Right now, scientists can use only some forms of matter in their quest—mostly hydrogen, the simplest *element.*

People called the first fusion weapon a hydrogen bomb because hydrogen was its key ingredient.

Einstein's equation gave early 20th-century scientists the idea that maybe the sun operated through some similar reaction—a reaction that somehow turned a little bit of matter into a lot of energy. That would explain how the sun could be its observed size yet last so long—10 million times longer than coal would burn—and seemed so unchanged over eons.

Physicists came to believe that the sun combined four *hydrogen* atoms—the simplest element in the universe—to make *helium*, the second-simplest substance in the universe. That's because helium is almost exactly four times heavier than hydrogen. But in science, it's the little details that are interesting. A scientist doing painstaking experiments in his laboratory found that, time after time, one helium atom weighed a tiny bit less than four hydrogen atoms.

Another scientist speculated that this missing mass—the "mass defect," scientists called it—might have been converted, as Albert Einstein had proposed a few years earlier, to energy.

Perhaps, in other words, hydrogen atoms forced to combine because of the sun's huge gravity—like a huge hand pressing its own atoms together, generating higher pressures and temperatures till some fused—did not have quite the mass they should have had because that missing little bit was being released as energy. Calculations by other scientists showed this seemed to be correct. It is this released energy, occurring a staggering number of times a second over the surface of the sun, that we call fusion energy, or nuclear fusion.

Calculations by scientists, who were more and more excited, showed that this reaction within the sun could explain the immense energy it sent out from its core and the longevity of its presence in the center of our solar system.

Nobel laureate physicist Hans Bethe is usually credited with putting all of this together, though many people contributed the bits that made his theory possible.

Starlight: The emitted energies of stars all are courtesy of nuclear fusion. (Courtesy NASA)

Early in the 20th century, scientists doing clever experiments using magnets and electricity found that atoms were not solid like marbles but could be considered to be made of *protons*, *electrons*, and *neutrons*. Protons have a positive electric charge, electrons (the stuff of electricity) have a negative charge, and neutrons are, well, neutral: they have no charge. Scientists discovered these traits when they found that powerful magnets would bend a beam of protons one way and a

imagined as a proton plus an electron, weigh just a little more than protons.

Scientists calculated that if gravity's pressure fused atoms in very hot star furnaces called supernovas, more elements could be made than hydrogen and helium. All the elements in our world are just greater and greater combinations of protons and neutrons. So, when these components are fused by the great gravity and heat of supernovas, they would form iron and lithium

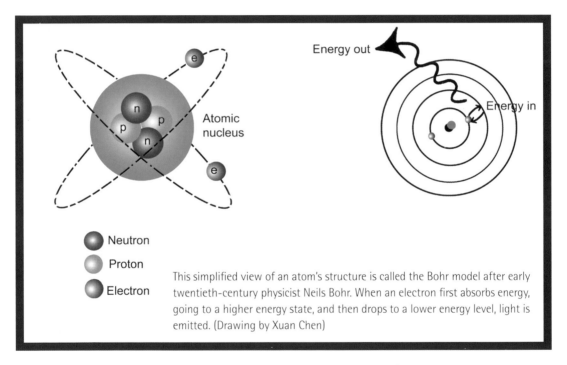

Neutron

Proton

Electron

This simplified view of an atom's structure is called the Bohr model after early twentieth-century physicist Neils Bohr. When an electron first absorbs energy, going to a higher energy state, and then drops to a lower energy level, light is emitted. (Drawing by Xuan Chen)

beam of electrons the other way. Later, neutrons were discovered to be unaffected by magnets.

A simple approximation of atoms: imagine electrons as lightweight little planets circling a huge sun made of protons and neutrons. Neutrons, which in very simple terms can be

and carbon and, under more extreme conditions, heavy elements like uranium and, in fact, ultimately all the atoms that make us humans. We are made of stuff created by stars.

From there, scientists realized two things: that all the stars in the sky, all the stars in the universe, probably ran on the energy created by nuclear fusion; and nuclear fusion could work to create more than helium, though hydrogen and helium make up 98 percent of the mass of our known universe. Greater pressures could combine more and more little atoms to make bigger and bigger atoms. The suns—including very hot suns called *supernovas*—made all the other elements that surround us.

And while this might have been considered "just a theory," scientists proved their theory when they created a hydrogen bomb—a method of forcing variations of hydrogen atoms to combine. When they did—a major achievement, in a way, of our little species— they sent out a terrific, a terrible amount of energy. It was the most destructive force humankind had ever liberated on earth. Fusion. Nuclear fusion. $E = mc^2$.

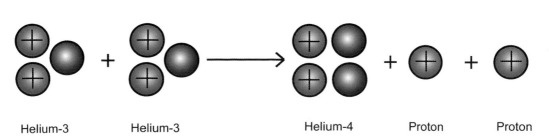

Proton   Proton   Deuteron   Positron

Deuteron   Proton   Helium-3

Helium-3   Helium-3   Helium-4   Proton   Proton

How does the sun change hydrogen nuclei (also known as protons) into helium? The steps include creation of a deuterium nucleus (a proton plus a neutron) essential to the fusion process, and a positron. A positron is a subatomic particle that weighs the same as an electron but has a positive electrical charge. (Drawing by Xuan Chen)

Well, but why mess with it further? Why the attempt to build huge machines that can produce this reaction? Nuclear fusion serves us pretty well by itself. Remember, almost every energy we know is born of the sun's strength. Plants grown by the sun's fusion energy eventually became coal and oil and gas. The sun of course is behind human solar energy efforts, which use sunlight either to warm water or air directly or to convert it into electricity. Wind occurs because energy from the sun warms the earth unevenly. The world is hotter at the equator, on which the sun shines directly, than it is at the North or South Pole, which the sun only hits obliquely, a kind of glancing impact. Also, shifting clouds block the sun from hitting some of the land. The different temperatures cause the air to move because hot air rises and cold air sinks. This creates pressure differences that Nature tries to equalize by redistributing air. We call it wind. We already use wind to turn big windmills that convert that motion of air into electricity. But it all comes from the action of the sun, which in its starring role also makes sunlight that lets us see and warms us.

So if fusion and its results are all around us, why do we want more of it?

We want it because we need electric power. We can't do without it, and even if we could, there are the huge populations of China and India and others in Africa and Asia that want it. The Chinese and Indian brothers and sisters number in the billions. Everybody wants to be able to turn on lights at night rather than sit in the dark. People don't want to haul water by hand, they want it pumped right into their houses; that takes electricity. People want to see other places in the world on their TV sets, listen to music on their i-Pods, watch movies on their DVD player or in movie theaters. They want mobile phones or house phones, x-rays and exercise machines, elevators and electric heaters, washing machines and dryers, and automobiles and airplanes. They want computers. All these things, and many more, take power.

We get this power now from coal, oil, gas, wind, sun, and *nuclear fission* energy.

But we're going to run out of coal, oil, gas, and uranium eventually. Mining coal and sucking out oil also creates big holes in the earth. Burning these substances mucks up our atmosphere—or we need to spend large sums to create filters that block harmful emissions and then dispose of those filters. Wind and sun are terrific but expensive and erratic, and machines to harness them take up a lot of real estate. Nuclear fission could be dangerous. If a nuclear fission reaction gets out of control, we could have an explosion. And uranium is dangerous to mine. What to do with the processed uranium after it's been used is a problem too because it's *radioactive*. It really does glow in the dark—blue in water where the reactor rods of electricity-generating plants are stored—and it's dangerous for a long time.

That brings us to nuclear fusion—*fusion*, meaning to bring together. To fuse. We want to bring together atoms of hydrogen so that their nuclei join. It's very difficult to do this, even though atoms of hydrogen are very small.

Nuclear fission is different from nuclear fusion. Fission requires very big atoms—uranium or plutonium—because they're the easiest to split. Fusion requires very small atoms, because they're the easiest to combine. Fusion scientists now intend to use variations of the hydrogen atom along with another widely available element called lithium.

Cookbook nuclear fission: Send a neutron into an isotope of uranium and it will split, creating energy and byproducts. This method is used to create electric power by nuclear fission. Nuclear fission is an effective energy source but requires the mining of potentially harmful and ultimately long-lived radioactive materials. (Drawing by Xuan Chen)

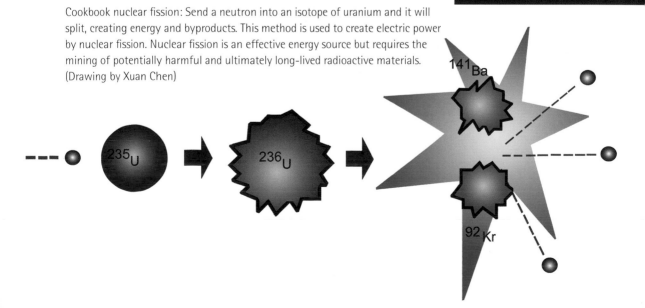

You might figure it can't be too tough to bully little atoms together. But they resist. It's like trying to bring the like ends of two magnets together. The closer you push them, the more they try to deflect away. So that's the problem with fusion: it's hard to do. If you can do it, the atoms release a lot of energy, which is what we want.

But a good thing about fusion being hard to do is that if anything goes wrong in a fusion power plant, the reaction will just stop. Unlike fission, which keeps on going like a car with a stuck accelerator, fusion just coasts to a stop. Because it's hard to make atoms fuse. If you stop forcing them, they just . . . stop combining. And it only takes water—actually, something called *heavy water*, which has more neutrons than regular water—to fuel the reaction.

So, every country could have a nuclear fusion reactor to make its own electricity. And the reactor would make electric power, and

Cookbook fusion: Two variants of the hydrogen ion merge to produce helium, neutrons, and energy. The two ions are deuterium, which is a hydrogen ion with an additional neutron in its nucleus, and tritium, a hydrogen ion with two neutrons in its nucleus. (Drawing by Xuan Chen)

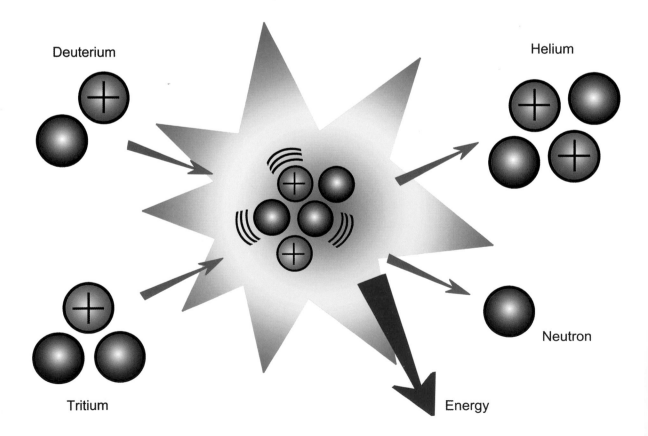

Deuterium

Helium

Tritium

Neutron

Energy

it wouldn't damage the atmosphere or hurt the earth, and nobody would have to fight for oil or other resources.

But it's very harrrrrrd to do.

On the other hand, it's amazing our three-pound (1.4 kilogram) human brains can control nature at this basic level to do it at all.

So, just to give us humans a pat on the back, I want to explain why it's amazing.

To do this, I need to talk a bit about time. If you're under, say, 20 years old, 100 years seems like a long time ago. And it should, because it's more than five times as long as you've been alive. Yet there are people—maybe your grandparents—who've been alive that long, or close to it. To them, if they're 80 or so, 100 years is not that long a time ago. The remaining 20 years is only one-fourth the time they've been alive, not five times as long, as it is for you. Time is relative.

But if 100 years is a long time ago, what about how long ago Jesus, Moses, Abraham, and the cave paintings existed, let alone the mass extinction 251 million years ago? Not to mention that scientists now believe the earth itself is 4.6 billion years old.

One hundred years ago doesn't seem so long compared to those times, does it? If you visualized all this time like a peach sliced in half, with 251 million years ago at the pit and the present as the skin, even your grandfather's 80- or 100-year-old life would be so thin a part of the skin that you couldn't even see it without a microscope. And your own 13 or 15 or 20 years—it's hardly imprinted there.

And yet it's in only this last 150 years—almost nothing in terms of time—that that little three-pound wrinkly control pod called the brain, which we all carry around in our skulls, has figured out how to control forces that gave you the world you grew up in.

Let's see what you wouldn't have had a mere 100 years ago. Your grandparents would know this from experience, but this is a reality check for you.

No Internet, right? No computers. No DVD players. No CDs. No phones. No electric lights. No radio.

People had to shop more often because there were no refrigerators (except for blocks of ice, delivered) and no electric freezers. People had to spend more time to get their clothes clean because there were no washing machines or dryers. Clothes had to be washed by hand—rubbed against the ribbings of washboards—and hung on clotheslines. No malls, because there were no cars. No air conditioning in the summer, no forced-air heating in the winter. No planes.

So a lot wasn't there 100 years ago, which is a very small time ago. And there were other major advances we haven't mentioned, like vaccinations against deadly diseases and giant modern tractors and reapers to more efficiently harvest food. But what do all these advances have in common?

They take electricity, at least in part. It takes electric power to heat, light, and run the precision labs that make medical advances or mass-produce huge harvesting machines. It takes a lot of power to run clocks and lights and microwaves and toasters and cars and planes. And that's a big problem. To get you—yes, you—all this stuff, all these choices, all this health and possibilities of vacationing in Santa Fe or Taos or Fort Lauderdale or Spain or Thailand, we need energy.

Most scientists believe that because humans, their transportation, and their industries are burning more fossil fuel every year, the earth is getting warmer. The ice caps are melting. If we don't do something, the next mass extinction may feature *us*.

This book is about fusion—the bringing together of atomic nuclei—to make energy safely.

The fusion we're talking about happened before food or music. Scientists think that 14 billion years ago—a billion is a thousand million—something small but very dense exploded and tiny pieces of matter raced out in all directions. Those little pieces, over many years, began to clump together. And when they clumped together big enough to be the size of stars, their atoms began to fuse and give off energy. They lit that star up. And so it is today. And that's how our sun fires up: as atoms combine because of the huge *gravity* and heat of our sun, they give off energy from nuclear fusion. That's what we call sunshine.

How much gravity does it take to create nuclear fusion? Scientists estimate the minimum gravity to create nuclear fusion naturally would be an object at least one-tenth the mass of our sun. That's why Jupiter—the largest planet in our solar system—is still just a planet. It's only about one-thousandth the size of our sun. It too could be a small, faint star if it were a hundred times bigger.

That's how it happens in stars. Cosmic blending. Fusion.

Even though on earth we don't have the huge mass of the stars to help fuse atomic nuclei, we want to use our three-pound brains and the little we've learned about electricity and magnetism over the last 150 years to make peacetime, environmentally safe fusion happen on earth.

We don't quite know how to do it yet.

We're trying a number of methods on this huge problem.

Talk about David fighting Goliath.

But who won that fight?

80130

The Z machine ready for cleaning, with its oil bath (between the outer and middle ring) and water bath (between inner ring and hub) emptied. Oil and water serve as insulation for cables carrying huge currents of electricity, the same way that plastic coatings insulate household electric lines to lamps, radios, and so on. The catwalks permit technicians to tend the machine. The empty cylinder near the top of this photo (but actually in the center of the machine) is where Z's tiny targets are placed. (Courtesy Sandia National Laboratories; photographer Randy Montoya)

Opposite: This cutaway of Z details the way electricity gets from its perimeter—the outside of the "wagon wheel" shape—to the hub that contains the target. (Drawing by Xuan Chen)

CHAPTER 2

The Z Machine's Lightning Bolt

The sun's huge gravity pulls its atoms together like a huge wrestler knocking heads. Some atoms collide and fuse, releasing energy.

The sun stays hot by keeping some of this energy inside itself. It releases the rest. Some of that energy reaches us on earth.

On earth, we don't have a huge gravitational field to help us make fusion. So we have to be clever. We need to use what we've discovered in the last 150 years.

The *Z machine*, at Sandia National Laboratories in Albuquerque, New Mexico, uses electricity and magnetism to create nuclear fusion.

Z sits silently at night, almost vacantly, like a person with something else on its mind. It forms a circle 108 feet (33 meters) in diameter and 20 feet (six meters) high. The yellow overhead lights shine on its huge presence like the lights in an old-fashioned gymnasium illuminate a basketball court after everyone has gone home.

Pools of water and oil bathe and insulate Z's 36 electrical transmission lines.

Looked down at from the ceiling, the machine resembles a huge wagon wheel.

Its rim is formed by large boxes called *capacitors* that store electricity.

Thirty-six electrical transmission lines are arranged like spokes. They connect the rim of the machine to its hub—a sealed vacuum chamber about 10 feet (three meters) in diameter and 20 feet (six meters) high.

With the throw of a switch, 26 million *amperes* will race through transmission lines as big around as a horse's girth, into the hub, and there, into a piece of equipment about as small as a spool of thread.

This "spool," called a *wire array*, features hundreds of very thin wires, an inch or so long, hung vertically. The thickness of each wire is about one-seventh the diameter of one of the hairs on your head, so thin that they're

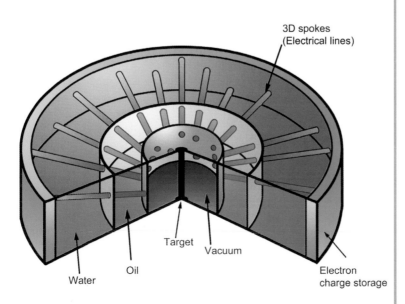

3D spokes
(Electrical lines)

Target
Vacuum
Water
Oil
Electron
charge storage

hard to see unless the light is just right. Usually, the wires are made of tungsten, like the filament of an Edison lightbulb. Tiny copper weights attached at their bottoms hold them straight. Otherwise, they would curl like hair having a bad day. They're very delicate and break easily.

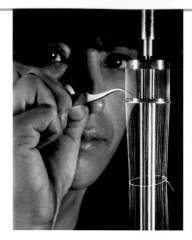

Just beyond the wires, a little oven called a *hohlraum* might be placed. It looks like a tiny soup can made of gold. Inside it, scientists place a capsule about the size of a BB. It's the material in that capsule—a form of hydrogen—that scientists want Z to compress until that material fuses and releases energy.

But that's for later. Those wires, the hohlraum, and the capsule won't even be loaded until the researchers are ready to fire a "shot." For now, all is quiet. The machine is sleeping. In the morning, the humans will come and goad it into action.

How much current passes through Z in the instant of its firing, compared with the amount used by a typical home? The main circuit breaker box in most US homes is usually wired to receive from 100 to 200 amps. If we take 26,000,000—the amount of current shooting along Z's transmission lines—and divide it by 200—the maximum capability of most houses—the result is that Z transmits approximately 130,000 times the amperage of a typical home. But only for 100 nanoseconds, or billionths of a second.

It's morning. At the hub of the wheel, a team of technicians dressed in white coveralls crouch in the 20-foot (six-meter)-deep hole at the center of Z. They're affixing the target, only about as big as a spool of thread, with wires almost too fine to be seen, with the hohlraum and capsule within it that will be the target of the energy pulse.

The machine's immense vitality will destroy the wires when it fires, like a *short circuit* of a car's battery melts a fuse or the way a tungsten filament can burn out in a lightbulb. But this destruction will happen a lot faster. Z, when it fires, produces hundreds of thousands of *volts*, not just the few of a car battery, in addition to its huge number of amps.

But the firing moment is still 15 minutes away. The technicians pack up their tools, leaving behind monitoring instruments with odd shapes and extreme angles usually seen only in science-fiction movies, and an orange light begins to flicker over doors, and people slightly hasten their progress toward the exits. And now there's almost no one in the Z machine's part of the building, which is a good thing because lights over each exit start revolving and they are red, and a siren goes off that arouses the adrenaline of anyone with ears. Nerves in every human brain signal that they don't want to be in that building at this time anymore. And then the doors are locked and the count up begins. "Ten . . . 20 . . . 30 . . . 60 . . . fully armed." There is a pause while cameras on the roof and throughout the building are monitored for signs of intruders, willful or ignorant . . . "FIRE!"

The ground shakes. A fireball reaching more than two million degrees is created for about five nanoseconds at Z's heart.

Try stamping the ground with your foot and see how close a friend has to stand to feel it. The Z shot can be felt in buildings hundreds of feet away from its source.

Opposite, top: Sandia technician Dolores Graham creates the tiny wire array structure through which 26 million amps will pass. Each wire is about one-seventh the diameter of a human hair. The working part of the array lies between the two horizontal metal plates. (Courtesy Sandia National Laboratories; photographer Randy Montoya)

Opposite, bottom: Workers prepare the central cylinder of Z to receive a target. Dust and stray metallic particles are bad. (Courtesy Sandia National Laboratories; photographer Randy Montoya)

Below: A partial view of Z's surface as it fires. The surface of Z is now plated over to bear the weight of instruments analyzing Z's power and other attributes, so this view is no longer available. (Courtesy Sandia National Laboratories; photographer Randy Montoya)

Z has a cool name—an end-of-days sound—but the name doesn't mean it's the ultimate machine at the end of time. It's really just a mathematical thing. You know from geometry class there is an *x*- and *y*-axis flat along your desk? So *z* is the vertical direction up from your desk? The basic reaction of the Z machine takes place in the vertical direction of a cylinder at the heart of the machine. This action is called a Z *pinch*. Thus, the Z machine.

But . . . what is a Z pinch?

To understand that, accept this basic rule of electricity: every electric current generates a magnetic field that wraps around it. There is even a rule, called the right-hand rule, that tells the direction the magnetic field coils around the wire.

A modern Z pinch works by passing a large electric current through hundreds of ultra-thin wires that resemble a wire cage. The current vaporizes the wires. That is, the wires burn out like electrical fuses zapped by too much electricity passing through them. But they don't really disappear. They become a gas of metallic *ions* and electrons called a *plasma*.

Remember the magnetic field that always surrounds an electric current? Even though the wires are no longer there, for a fraction of a second, the electricity flows through the electrons still present in the plasma. So the magnetic field remains. And it has the ions in its grasp.

The magnetic field substitutes for the sun's gravitational field. But instead of bringing together hydrogen ions over millions of years, the magnetic field brings together wire-array ions in nanoseconds.

Like a hand closing into a fist, the powerful magnetic field pinches together the cloud of ions, reducing them from the thickness of a spool of thread to the thickness of pencil lead. The closer to the *z*-axis the ions are, the more energy the ions receive and the faster they accelerate.

When the ions reach the central axis, they can't go any farther. Ions are coming at the center from every direction, like cavalry racing in from every direction to reach a single vertical line. There, they brake to a sudden stop. Because they are going very fast, they have a lot of energy. They release that energy like a fast-moving car slamming into a brick wall or like the heat from brakes jammed on at high speed. But these ions are moving a lot faster than the car. And they stop in a far shorter distance. So they release their energy in a much shorter period of time, emitting a huge burst of power in the form of x-rays, a very intense energy.

These x-rays are the same as the ones you receive in a dental office. But those come in tiny doses.

Artist's conception of ions reduced to a plasma and magnetically contracted to form the core of a Z-pinch. The arrows heading for the exits represent x-rays formed as the wire plasma is forced to brake to a stop at the center of the pinch. (Courtesy Sandia National Laboratories)

Pretend to grip an electric wire in your right hand. The magnetic field around the wire flows in the direction of your fingers.

If someone punches you in the shoulder, it hurts. A "live" electric wire shocks if you touch it. A magnet holds on to iron just like a hand grabbing a shoulder.

But what makes action happen when nothing touches?

First, can that even happen? If someone shoots out his hand and stops a few inches from your shoulder, he hasn't hurt you. And if a hand isn't gripping a shoulder, it can't hold on.

But if you put iron filings on a piece of paper and put a magnet below the paper, the filings—not touching the magnet at all—will arrange themselves in an order that looks like they are trying to form rings.

If you rub a piece of paper on the fur of a cat and put the paper on a metal pot (without your fingers touching the pot) on a table, the paper will become electrified. Shredded paper placed below it on the table will shift position or even fly up to it.

Why do these things happen?

Something—some force—must be passing invisibly through space to cause the iron filings or shredded paper to move.

Spooky action at a distance: the first is an example of a magnetic field and the second, of an electric field.

Before 1830—just two centuries ago, roughly speaking—no one suspected such fields existed. It was a new idea, a new understanding, of invisible forces.

Magnetic and electric fields are very important to creating fusion on earth.

Z releases very large doses—approximately 200 terawatts (trillion watts)—in x-ray power. (By comparison, all the energy producers in the world generate approximately 20 terawatts in any given moment.)

That's a Z pinch.

It's a lot of power. But by itself, Z can't solve our energy problems. Remember that the power released by the Z pinch, while very large, is only available for a few nanoseconds.

So keep reading.

To achieve nuclear fusion, we have to go a step further.

These x-rays are emitted into a gold chamber, the hohlraum. The tiny chamber, although it looks like a soup can, actually functions like a small oven. Inside the hohlraum, which is beyond what—nanoseconds ago—used to be a wire array, is the BB-size capsule. The x-rays, bouncing around in the hohlraum, are going to cook that capsule like an oven cooks a turkey.

Inside the capsule is a material called *deuterium*, an *isotope* of hydrogen. The x-rays are going to pound on the exterior capsule wall. A strange thing happens. The x-rays blast the sphere's exterior so intensely that they ablate, or boil away, its surface material. The material departs in the form of hot gases just like the exhaust of a rocket.

The forceful emission of gas drives the interior of the capsule in the opposite direction. Because the capsule is a sphere with gases shooting outward in every direction, the deuterium stuffing of the capsule is driven inward, shrinking into a smaller and smaller ball. As it does, some of the deuterium nuclei will fuse, creating nuclear fusion. Energy comes out in the form of neutrons, which we'll talk about in a bit. (The energy could be converted later to electricity in a steam generator.)

This process is called *inertial confinement*. Inertia is the quality that tends to keep a body moving once it's in motion. That's why a rolling car is hard to stop: it has inertia. Inertia also makes it hard to get a stopped object moving. (Ever try to push a stalled car?)

Inertia at Z helps keep the deuterium nuclei together. A *fuel capsule* is *imploded* so quickly that the inertia of the converging *ions* causes fusion to occur before—like a decompressing spring—they have a chance to bounce back out.

The term *inertial confinement* might seem useless to memorize. But it's important to know because it contrasts with the other main method used by humans to create fusion. That is called *magnetic confinement*. A cloud of very hot, rapidly moving ions is contained by a powerful magnetic field so they can't escape and may fuse.

We'll come to that powerful technique two chapters from now.

But whether inertial or magnetic, the common word in both methods is *confinement*. Hydrogen ions don't want to fuse. They want to be free. So they have to be controlled—contained somehow—so that they don't run off.

Scientists at Z do this by putting them in a little capsule and using x-rays from an imploded wire array to force them together.

The overall term to describe Z's operation is *pulsed power*. That's because Z delivers its power in a burst, like an explosion. In fact, the Z machine's main purpose is to provide data to simulate atomic weapons. That means the US government doesn't need to actually explode a nuclear bomb to get test data; scientists instead can fire the Z machine and use that data to simulate the rest—accurately, scientists hope, and harmlessly.

But note that the term is *pulsed power*, not *pulsed energy*.

This is because energy is a timeless quantity, like a mountain lake stored behind a dam.

If you let water from the lake empty in a trickle, it won't even turn a water wheel. A lot of potential energy is there but not enough power.

Power is the amount of energy let out over some time period.

For example, if you suddenly remove the dam, there's a lot of power because all the water comes out in a few minutes. Not only will it turn the wheel, it may knock down a town in its path. It's the same lake, with the same energy. But energy released faster means more power.

Now, if you could get the same amount of water to come out in a billionth of a second, you would have a billion times the power of energy released in a second.

Z is like that.

Z is powerful, but not because it uses so much energy. A single firing at Z, in terms of energy, is the equivalent of only two or three sticks of dynamite. The energy it siphons from the electrical grid in about 90 seconds is only enough to light a few blocks of houses for a few minutes.

But it expends that energy in a very brief burst to create a Z pinch, which lasts for only 100 billionths of a second (100 nanoseconds). That's a lot of power during those nanoseconds.

Scientists playing at Z have learned it can do interesting tricks. The pressures of its magnetic field can melt diamond, the hardest substance on Earth.

They can very briefly create the type of ice found on the very cold planet Neptune—called Ice-7, not the same as Earth ice—and can be used to model the huge pressures at the core of the giant planet Jupiter.

The changing magnetic field can propel little disks through vacuum faster than Earth moves through space.

And Z's x-ray patterns can mimic the patterns found around black holes in space, helping astronomers study them.

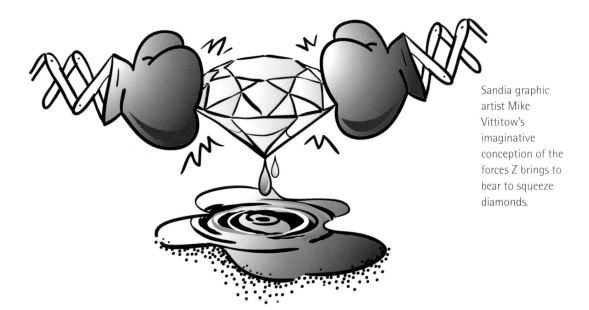

Sandia graphic artist Mike Vittitow's imaginative conception of the forces Z brings to bear to squeeze diamonds.

Now Z scientists want the method to do a very hard trick indeed: to fuse hydrogen atoms in a way that produces more energy than scientists put into the process. So scientists make a target of an isotope of the hydrogen atom called deuterium. The normal hydrogen nucleus consists of a proton. Deuterium is a hydrogen atom with a proton and a neutron in its nucleus. This version of hydrogen has twice as much mass as ordinary hydrogen because it has a neutron and a proton at its heart. When combined with oxygen (the same way that two ordinary hydrogen atoms and one oxygen form water—H_2O), the result is called "heavy water." Deuterium is found in seawater, one in every 6,000 atoms, and is readily available. It doesn't sound like much, but there's enough to deliver energy to humans for many centuries.

The Iceman Cometh: Researcher Daniel Dolan has used Z to compress water into ice at extreme temperatures and pressures. (Courtesy Sandia National Laboratories; photographer Randy Montoya)

Two isotopes of hydrogen are of interest in nuclear fusion. In addition to deuterium, another isotope of hydrogen is called *tritium*. It has two neutrons and a proton in the nucleus. Tritium is an isotope that's hard to come by. It's unstable and has a very short life span—about 12.3 years—so it is very rarely found in nature. Humans who want it usually have to create it. (To help remember these names, think that *deu* means "two" and *tri* means "three.")

The deuterium and/or tritium nuclei, shoved together, release energy as they join to form a nucleus of the element helium, which is very stable. This nucleus is so important that it has its own name: an *alpha particle*.

Why are these isotopes so good at combining?

Ordinarily, nuclei of hydrogen atoms repel each other because they are protons, each positively charged. It's hard to make them combine.

Still, because hydrogen nuclei have fewer protons than all other atoms, they have less positive charge, so it's easier to push them together.

Furthermore, hydrogen atoms (like other atoms) have no defense against neutrons entering their nuclei because neutrons have no charge.

Once a neutron joins a hydrogen nucleus, the resultant deuterium isotope has the same positive charge as a hydrogen atom but twice the mass over which that charge is distributed. So the charge protecting the nucleus isn't as effective.

This is even truer of tritium, which has the same electric charge as a hydrogen atom distributed over approximately three times the mass.

So these nuclei can combine more easily. When they do, they form helium and release energy in the form of neutrons. (They also release other particles that don't concern us here.) Some of the released neutrons enter the nuclei of other hydrogen atoms, making these more likely to combine with still other atoms to release still more energy. Tritium greases the reaction process because it has two neutrons instead of only one.

Theoretically, if you could get the capsule hot enough and compressed enough so that these fusion reactions continued on their own after an initial push from Z, you would have a capsule that would yield more energy than has been put into it. That would be high-yield hydrogen fusion. That's what we want. No one has done this yet at Z.

At Z, engineers load up electricity onto the plates, called capacitors, around Z's outer wall. The electricity comes from a circuit in the wall. Getting it is like plugging in a lamp at home, except at Z we're just storing the electricity to use as power instead of heating a filament to produce light.

Electrical charge can be stored on a metal plate like peanut butter on a slice of bread. The plate is half of a capacitor. The capacitor stores electricity. When another plate is brought close enough, a waterfall (in a sense) is created in terms of the difference in voltage between the charged and uncharged plates. The stored electric charge actually jumps to the other plate, ready to move through any attached wire to do work in the outer world.

Z uses 26 million amps. It drives them forward over a "waterfall" of hundreds of thousands of volts. So we're talking a lot of watts. All of this is ejected suddenly in one millisecond (a thousandth of a second) from the capacitors on the rim of the machine. This mighty current burns its way along 36 transmission lines to the center of the machine. Switches shorten the pulse from milliseconds to about 200 nanoseconds (billionths of a second), then through a device that gives the energy pulse shape and shortens it to 100 nanoseconds. The x-rays formed by this pulse hit their target in only five nanoseconds. The pulse, in short, goes through a series of compressions in a very small amount of time to dramatically increase its power.

So those little thin wires at the heart of Z are doomed.

Let's think about this. In a car, which runs on a 12-volt battery and a few amps, you can see fuses in their box, usually near the dashboard. They are short, thin strips of metal, readily

Opposite, left: Marcus Knudsen examines the fort-like structure he places at the heart of Z when the machine is used to test materials under extreme conditions. Accelerated by the machine's huge magnetic fields, tiny projectiles accelerated to speeds far faster than a rifle bullet will smash into targets inserted in the two circular holes, revealing otherwise unobtainable information about the behavior of materials under stress. (Courtesy Sandia National Laboratories; photographer Randy Montoya)

Opposite, right: Marcus Knudson stands at the perimeter of Z's vacuum chamber, into which the test structures he holds will be inserted. (Courtesy Sandia National Laboratories; photographer Randy Montoya)

An ion is an atom with too few or too many electrons. Normally the negatively charged electrons and the positively charged nucleus balance each other out. The atom sits there like a car in neutral, doing relatively little. But lose or gain an electron and it's a different story. The atom has become a bad boy. Unlike an atom, an ion is easily influenced. Its electric charge makes it more vulnerable to influences from magnetic fields. Z's massive electric current altered the metal atoms of the wires and turned them into ions. Now they are free-floating in a gas cloud, sensitive to magnetic forces that they weren't before.

Their electrons, free-floating, are better carriers of electricity than ever before.

visible. If there's a short circuit, which means much too much current is traveling down toward your disc player or horn or lights than intended, the purpose of the fuse is to disappear. It burns out. It vaporizes. Then the electricity can't travel onward because there's no metal for it to travel through. This protects the car's electrical parts until the two wires causing the short circuit are separated and a new fuse is put in.

But in Z, we're talking about wires much thinner than a fuse. They're so fine you can hardly see them. And all of Z's massive current—26 million amps—across a huge voltage drop—hundreds of thousands of volts—must go through these wires. Didn't these scientists realize what would happen? There's going to be a short circuit. The wires are going to burn out, sure as anything! Stop!!

Imagine Wile E. Coyote (from the cartoon) charging along the wire in the direction of the current, determined to catch that Roadrunner up ahead. Suddenly, there are no more wires under him. They dissolve. But Coyote doesn't know that there are no more wires. He's fine until—as in the cartoon—he looks down and sees nothing supporting him. Then he lets out a wail and begins to fall . . .

In fact, the wires do burn out. But a funny thing happens as they do. As the wires heat up, they don't simply disappear. Their atoms boil off the surface of wire and ionize into a plasma of electrons and ions. The electrons of a plasma, free of the constraints of operating within a rigid wire, conduct electricity even better than before. For nanoseconds, the magnetic field becomes even stronger, pulling the ions into the center of the cylinder at an ever-accelerating pace, faster than Wile E. Coyote has ever fallen in his life.

Wile E. Coyote begins his very fast fall, accelerating toward the center of the field, which is the vertical axis of the spool of thread. The magnetic field contracts like a fist closing, and it closes very fast. We talked about the speed of light. This fist closes at a considerable fraction of the speed of light. An airplane moving that fast would take you from San Francisco to New York in a few seconds. And in the grip of that magnetic field, vulnerable to it because they have an electric charge, are the ions of the plasma.

Hasta la vista, Wile E. Coyote. If we could look down on this scene from above, as though we were in an airplane looking down on a football game, at first we would have seen a vertical curtain of wires hanging on the rim of something resembling a spool of thread, an inch or so in diameter. Now the wires, transformed into ions, are being rushed inward in the grip of the magnetic hand closing until their perimeter reaches about the thickness of pencil lead.

And now there's nowhere farther for them to go. The ones coming from any part of the circle meet the ions coming toward them from the other side, like a bunch of cars all heading from the perimeter of a circle to its center. Either they come to a sudden stop or they smash.

Have you ever touched the tires of a car after it stops suddenly? They're hot. They don't look hot, they look the same, but you can feel the heat if you put your hand close by.

But these cars were only going about 60 or 70 miles an hour (97 or 113 kilometers an hour) and it took 10 seconds or so to stop them. The ions travel tens of thousands of miles a second and they stop in trillionths of a second. So they're realllly hot! So hot that instead of giving off heat in the *infrared* range, which is what tires emit—the same as an iron pot that turns cherry red from heat on a stove—these particles give off much more energetic heat as they stagnate. This heat is in the form of x-rays, which is just another form of energy.

The little box under the finger of Sandia National Laboratories researcher Daniel Sinars contains a crystal that, like sunglasses, only allows certain frequencies of light to pass through. The method Sinars developed for Z gave sight to scientists formerly blinded by the maelstrom of energies otherwise swirling in the machine when it fires. (Courtesy Sandia National Laboratories; photographer Randy Montoya)

All forms of energy are cousins. X-rays are just much more intense than infrared rays.

But there's nothing "just" about the amount of power given off in x-rays in this Z pinch. It is equal to many times the electric power produced by all the electrical-generating power plants on earth!

So is this fusion? Are we there yet? No way!

The Z pinch produces this energy for a hundred nanoseconds. That's not very long but long enough to produce x-rays that take five nanoseconds to smash into the surface of a nearby, BB-size, spherical capsule. The impact causes the exterior of the shell to rocket off. The inner part of the shell, by Newton's law of equal and opposite reaction, shoots farther inward, compressing the hydrogen and squeezing its interior to fusion conditions of temperature and pressure.

Some of these hydrogen isotopes, driven inward, smash into each other at high speed. They combine, releasing energy in the form of neutrons (and particles called neutrinos, which don't interact).

But there are always interesting problems along the way. To fuse most of the deuterium atoms in the capsule (at this writing, no one at Z has used tritium), the capsule must be compressed evenly on all sides. That is, the pellet can't behave like a water balloon that pops out between your fingers when you squeeze it. Instead it must compress evenly everywhere around its surface.

Then deuterium atoms can't escape.

Some fuse, releasing (among other subatomic particles) energetic neutrons, a sign of the fusion of isotopes of hydrogen.

In 2003, scientists at Z reported the mighty feat that they had been able to evenly shrink a pellet of deuterium. Not far enough to make *high-yield fusion*, which is what they want. That would mean a reaction that combines so many atoms that it puts out far more energy than researchers put into it. The reaction would be so hot, and so many neutrons would be re-entering other deuterium atoms to produce energy and helium, that almost all the deuterium would be used up in Z's short firing burst.

That's what humanity needs to get electric power from this reaction.

What Z had shown was only that it was possible to create fusion neutrons using pulsed power. They had been able to deliver enough power to a capsule to cause some fusion. The amount of fusion was the first baby step of a new contender in the race for controlled nuclear fusion.

But how did all this work on Z and fusion come about?

Turn the page.

Opposite: The amount of capsule compression needed to produce ignition through the method of inertial fusion. The BB-size starting capsule is represented by the basketball; the black dot represents the size of the capsule relative to the basketball. The ratio is about 30:1. Both Z and laser fusion efforts have achieved approximately 20:1 as of this writing. (Image provided by Sandia scientist Mike Cuneo)

One of Isaac Newton's laws of motion can be easily seen in a game of pool or billiards. A cue ball hitting another ball transfers part of its momentum to the other ball. Hit hard, both balls leave the area of intersection in two different directions. This is the same principle that drives a rocket forward. The force of the burning jet fuel shooting rearward drives the rocket forward with a momentum equal to that possessed by the escaping gases.

Atoms for a time were thought of as solar systems, like our sun and its planets. Like many things in physics, we don't really know this. It was just a useful image. The concept explained in a simplified manner how atoms behave, and so physicists used it early on like this:

Electrons are small and circle the sun like planets; they have a negative charge. The "sun," or nucleus, is made up of much heavier protons and neutrons, clumped together in the center of the circling electrons. The protons have a positive charge that balances out the negative charge of the electrons. That means the atom is electrically neutral. This is called the Bohr model of the atom, after the physicist who theorized it, Niels Bohr.

Neutrons have no charge. In a simplified sense, a neutron can be considered to be built of one proton and one electron. The charges cancel each other, but because the electron is so light, a neutron weighs only a tiny bit more than a proton. Still, protons and neutrons have far different properties. To create nuclear fusion through means we currently think achievable, it turns out we must be able to release neutrons.

CHAPTER 3
Z's Alpha and Omega

CSI and other TV crime shows use scientific techniques to bring criminals to justice. The scientific approach used to catch crooks and "deviants" has fascinated audiences since Sherlock Holmes. It's a little dash of science in the overall game of cops and robbers.

But people with really exciting inner lives aren't satisfied with using just a dash of science to search for a murderer who usually at best is only moderately imaginative. Instead, they use science full time looking for clues to the secrets of the universe. They're looking for something no one has ever seen or thought. Each time scientists do this, proposing in some quiet technical paper new theories about forces never before recognized, they achieve something more profound than corralling a thief. They drive worldwide ignorance back a little further.

Scientists found we live on a round planet that moves around the sun, not on one flat as a pizza that the sun passes over every day in a golden chariot.

It's hard to travel to other planets if your belief system doesn't let you think there are any.

It's hard to understand weather if you believe storms are up to the whim of some irresponsible deity puffing his cheeks and blowing.

Or electricity, if you think only Zeus has rights to lightning bolts.

As it is with our gradually improving understanding of the universe and the weather, so it is with Z. The machine didn't appear fully clothed, born perfect, as something for students to study. Rather, it started the way students do. It was an idea, and then it was a little tyke, and then it got bigger and now it's in its teenage years. And no one knows what it will ultimately make of its life. It was supposed to provide data to use in supercomputers to simulate the effects and vulnerabilities of nuclear weapons so that the bombs wouldn't have to be exploded to test them. That's a good idea, but the machine got more powerful than that. It attracted bigger ideas. Researchers thought that instead of just creating data imitating a nuclear bomb, its method could just possibly create enough fusion to make unlimited electric power from seawater. Will it be a success in this or just hang out like someone without a high school diploma trying to figure out what to do with its life? Despite all the science studied and all the money spent, no one knows.

But scientists keep working on it, bringing it forward a little bit every day.

In the 19th century, people learned that any electric current traveling along a wire was accompanied by a magnetic field.

In the 1950s, Malcolm Haines, former director of London's Imperial College Plasma Physics Department, predicted the conditions needed for the explosions of single wires and the amount of current (and thus, magnetic field) necessary in Z pinches to produce fusion.

In the 1980s, Valentin Smirnov, director of the Institute of Nuclear Fusion at the *Kurchatov Institute* in Moscow, proposed using puffs of gas instead of wires as a possible source of ions for Z pinches.

Researchers at Sandia studied the reaction.

It was known that vertically stringing 10 or 15 wires in a cylindrical array, or hanging an actual thin metal cylinder and then passing a large current through either, created ions. The magnetic field, associated with the vertical current that vaporized the metal, pinched the ions together. The researchers were able to extract x-ray power out of it, but it wasn't much. The speed of the reaction wasn't fast enough to generate the large amount of x-rays needed to make fusion. And so the technique remained only a curiosity.

Researchers tried increasing the number of wires from 10 to even 24 wires, but the amount of x-rays produced didn't vary much, and it was annoying to string the wires because they were so thin that they broke easily. The researchers didn't bother to go further. They assumed that the ions created by the individual wires formed one big field, like a shower curtain. More wires just made the shower curtain a tiny bit stronger. Nothing very exciting there.

(Remember from chapter 2: the idea is to send huge electric currents through the wires and turn them into a plasma that the force of magnetism implodes, creating x-rays that can heat a pellet of "heavy" hydrogen hot enough to create nuclear fusion.)

Only theorists from across the country at the Naval Research Laboratory suggested that using more wires might have an effect.

Until one young researcher—Tom Sanford—got a new instrument called a pinhole camera. A pinhole camera for kids can be made or bought on the Net. It's a box with an opening that light can enter. Film along the back wall registers the image (upside down) created by the light.

It's an old-fashioned idea. But this camera was a modern marvel. Its electronics permitted nanosecond exposures. An explosion couldn't shatter its lens because it had none. A subject merely was placed at the camera's focal length, where an object is in focus at a specific distance from the camera. Protected by shock-absorbing devices, it could be placed close to the wire array and take pictures of unequaled clarity.

With this camera, Sanford expected to photograph ions contracting like a cloud when Z fired and destroyed its own fragile target wiring.

What the young man saw stunned him.

Instead of the ions from the destroyed wires forming one big magnetic shell, the ions from each destroyed wire remained in place. Individual ion shells formed around the ghostlike remnants of each former wire. Each lurched inharmoniously inward, in the grip of the magnetic field, toward the center of the spool.

If each wire's ions is clumping like this, Sanford thought, *using only a few wires seems like a bad idea.*

Maybe, he thought, there should be 50 wires instead of 10 or 20. Maybe there should be 100 or more. Because if they were rushing the center individually, you didn't want any holes between them. And if it was their sudden stopping in the center that released energy, then the more wires, the bigger the output. Sanford wanted enough wires to form the solid wall of ions people mistakenly thought was already occurring.

So here now was the chance collision of training and fate. The young scientist wasn't just smart. He had studied physics with two Nobel laureates—Leon Lederman and Sam Ting. Most people accept that Nobel laureates are uncommonly intelligent, but there's more to it than that. They study their subject intensely. They try to miss no fact. They run countless experiments to show that something is wrong with what they thought was true because they don't want to mislead people or—equally bad if you have pride—have someone else show they are wrong. They read everything on their subject that they can. They're bulldogs. Once they grip on a subject, they don't let go, no matter how the material thrashes around in their jaws.

The young man had been trained by bulldogs.

They had taught him that the harder they worked, the "luckier" they got.

It was chance that Sanford was at Sandia at all. He had been on a flight that had a stopover in Albuquerque. He had seen a small sign in the airport advertising for physicists to come work at Sandia. Even though it wasn't the kind of physics he was trained for, he was interested in the challenge of the big machine. He applied and was accepted. He came to work. That was chance, or the hand of God, or however you care to look at it.

Tom Sanford grins, years later, from the scene of his earlier triumph at Sandia's Z machine. (Courtesy Sandia National Laboratories; photographer Bill Doty)

But to change Z's procedures so that it would run the experiments with more wires—that took tenacity. Convincing coworkers. Negotiations with management. It took being a bulldog. It was hard to string the wires without breaking them. It took time, and time was money. And why do it?

Yet one day, the experiment took place using 90 wires. It took place on a relatively small Sandia Z pinch machine called Saturn and immediately increased its output from 15 to 40 trillion watts (terawatts) of x-ray power. The power output was so much stronger than ever achieved before that people marveled.

The result led to an intense period of work by community-minded Sandia engineers. These included Gerry Yonas, Wendland Beezhold, Ray Leeper, John Maenchen, Tom Nash, Barry Marder, George Allshouse, Ray Mock, and Chris Deeney, all fascinated by the new capability and wanting to find precisely what made it work.

They used wires of different thicknesses and adjusted the spacing between them to keep the total wire mass constant. They wanted to determine whether wire size and wire spacing had an appreciable effect.

Z rising: When you own a stock, this is what you want to see happen to its price. Here, the innovation of using many tiny wires to carry current sharply increased the output of Z's predecessor machine Saturn, and then Z's into the 200-terawatt range. (Courtesy Sandia National Laboratories)

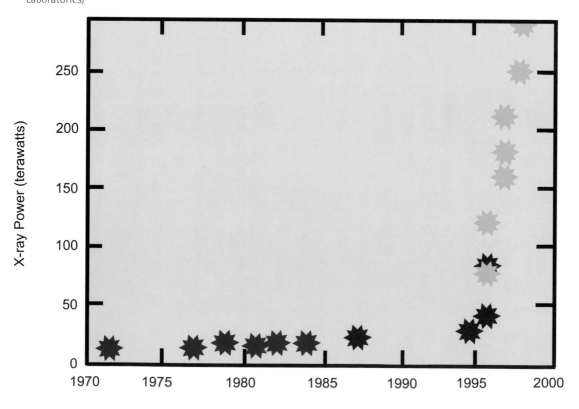

They soon produced an output of 80 trillion watts.

When the process was shifted over to Z (at that time, still called PBFA-II for an earlier method involving a particle beam), the machine's output soon exceeded 200 terawatts in output x-ray power, using arrays that numbered in the hundreds of wires.

As an additional bonus, the plasma pinch was more stable because the x-ray pulse shortened in time from 15 to three nanoseconds. (Plasma *instabilities* are the bugaboo of fusion efforts. They can cause sausage-like crimping to the shape of a cylindrical pinch and cause it to wink out without achieving its maximum power. The more time the reaction has, the more openings for instabilities.)

Plasma bugaboos: using a magnetic field to contain hot ions has its problems. What's wanted is a smooth cylindrical shape, not a hula dancer (a so-called kink instability) or a plasma with a succession of tight abs (sausage instability). Instabilities mean the plasma is unable to maintain itself and will shortly close down. (Drawing by Xuan Chen)

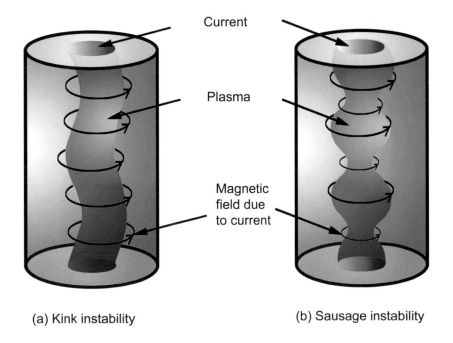

Current

Plasma

Magnetic field due to current

(a) Kink instability   (b) Sausage instability

The observations of Sanford and other Sandia researchers helped create the reality of a powerful Z pinch. That arrangement continues to be investigated to this day. It may one day be part of the method to produce electricity derived from controlled nuclear fusion.

But there are other problems.

These could be daunting.

As Keith Matzen, the director of Sandia's pulsed-power work, says of the effort taking place year after year after year, "Achieving nuclear fusion isn't for people who give up easily."

Searching for unlimited energy isn't like a TV show where everything wraps up at the end of the hour or a funny movie like *Ocean's Eleven*, which used a Z pinch machine carried in a van to short-circuit the lights of Las Vegas for a robbery. (No, it wouldn't work. And Z weighs thousands of tons, far too heavy to be carried in a van.)

First, as powerful as Z is, it must be much more powerful to create fusion. It's not just trying to knock over a casino. For a short moment, it's trying to create a miniature sun on earth, without help from a gravitational field. Its goal is to create high-yield nuclear fusion—the goal of all fusion-for-power projects. It would be the goal of humanity, if everyone understood it.

As of this writing, the input current to Z is 26 million amps.

But what theory tells us is needed is 60 million amps—a huge army of electrons marching through wiring. More than any machine on earth currently uses.

Sixty million amps, it is thought, could create powerful enough ions and x-rays to compress a pellet of heavy water enough that we would get much more energy out than we put in.

How is that possible? Where does the extra energy come from?

Everyone knows that you can't get more energy out of a machine than you put into it. You stop pedaling, it stops moving.

So why does so much energy result from nuclear fusion?

It's because atoms already have energy inside them from the way they were built in stars. When we alter them to a less intense form, we release the energy that held their components in place, just as (in the much less powerful chemical reaction) when we burn gasoline to reduce it to exhaust fumes, we release more energy than a gallon of the innocent-looking fluid appears to have.

So we need a power plant more than twice as big as any we have now to try this, unless scientists can come up with cheaper, better ways to produce x-rays to compress the pellet and release neutrons.

Lasers that could preheat the capsule—giving it a kind of jump-start—might help. Sandia's Z-beamlet laser may be up the task.

But even if fusion could be reliably achieved every day, it's not yet the end of the quest. A machine that creates fusion using pulses of power needs to fire frequently to run a power plant. For a machine like Z to create energy as the heart of a power plant, it has to fire every 10 seconds. Right now, it fires only once or twice a day.

A technician holds one of the optical pieces of Sandia's Z-beamlet laser. The amplified light passes through the large tubes near him. The laser, one of the most powerful in the world, takes x-ray snapshots of what's going on at Z's target as the machine fires. Plans include using the laser to pre-heat fusion pellets to hasten Z's entry into fusion conditions. (Courtesy Sandia National Laboratories; photographer Randy Montoya)

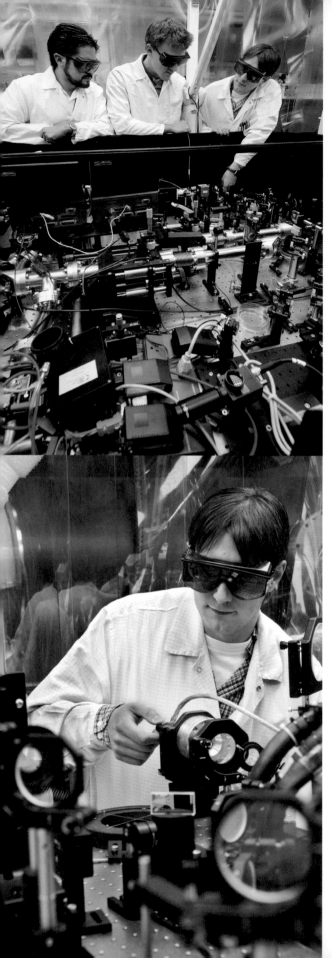

But help is on the way. It's called an LTD (linear transformer device; don't worry about the name). It's shaped like a donut. It's about 10 feet (three meters) across and one foot (0.3 meter) thick, and its capacitors and switches easily can put out pulses of one million amps and 100,000 volts that last only millionths of a second.

Developed initially in Siberia with a longer pulse by Russians Boris Kovalchuk and Sasha Kim, the time length of the pulse was shortened under the leadership of Sandia's Dillon McDaniel.

Mike Mazarkis, also at Sandia, then created a system that could charge the donut, fire it, and then remove the exhaust every 10 seconds. So, a shorter pulse, fired rapidly.

Sandia is testing these devices hooked in series with each other to see if their action works well together.

The advantages of LTDs are that the fast pulse they emit doesn't require the complicated switching and oil- and water-bath insulation of the current version of Z. Furthermore, the devices fire in the midrange of their capability, which promises well for their endurance. (If you're working at your peak every time you perform, as does the current version of Z, you'll probably bust something sooner than later.) One LTD device tested at Sandia fired every 10 seconds more than 13,000 times before it was turned off to make room for other experiments.

Opposite, top: Poor man's laser-beam corrector—contractors Daniel Headley (left) and Marc Ramsey (center), with Sandia researcher Jens Schwarz, examine the performance of an optical clamp they developed that cheaply corrects for laser beam distortion in Sandia's Z-beamlet laser. (Courtesy Sandia National Laboratories; photographer Randy Montoya)

Opposite, bottom: Jens Schwarz checking for laser beam distortion at Z-beamlet. The laser here functions like a dental x-ray machine. Its light strikes a plate that releases x-rays, just as Z fires. It is images taken by these x-rays that tell scientists how much the fusion capsule has shrunk. (Courtesy Sandia National Laboratories; photographer Randy Montoya)

From Siberia, not Area 51 (where some people believe the government stores alien flying saucers): Sandia researcher Bill Fowler tests circuits on an LTD device built in Tomsk and modified at Sandia. This machine is able to produce large electrical pulses rapidly and repeatedly. Rapid firing is necessary for inertial fusion machines to drive electrical generating plants, the same way an automobile's engine cylinders must fire rapidly and continuously to move the car forward. (Courtesy Sandia National Laboratories; photographer Randy Montoya)

Why does the huge machine have to fire rapidly, over and over again? Imagine a car engine cylinder firing one day and then a second explosion the next day. This won't push a car forward very fast. It might be a week before you left your block, if you were lucky.

Similarly, for Z to create electric power, its firings must come often enough to keep heating water (or some other fluid) into steam that turns a turbine to produce electricity.

This process spins a magnet to create varying magnetic fields in nearby pieces of iron. This induces an electric current in wires coiled around the pieces of iron—the reverse of using an electric current to create a magnetic field. A magnetic field moving across wires creates an electric current in those wires. That simple process is what creates all the electricity driving your home's lights and machines.

Another problem is containment. What material can contain the sun? Unlike the result of exploding a mixture of gasoline and air in a metal cylinder, the fusion reaction is the most powerful reaction known to humanity. What would contain not just one explosion, which regularly destroys the three-eighths-inch steel that contains it, but the reactions occurring every 10 seconds?

Scientists, in a plan developed by retired Sandian Craig Olson, currently envision a carousel on which targets of Z travel. The targets hang from a kind of metal clothesline and travel around a long oval like plaster horses on a merry-go-round. At the firing point, where Z is delivering a huge electric pulse every 10 seconds, a target—the wire array, hohlraum, and deuterium-tritium capsule—drops into a cylinder filled with an impact-muffling substance like vermiculite—a cousin of the plastic beads used to protect delicate contents of shipped packages. The vermiculite absorbs energy from the explosion and then releases its heat through a metal wall to water (or some other fluid) passing through a pipe. The fluid turns to steam. Then the carousel moves forward, lifting out the container and putting another one in its stead. The whole process begins again. A robot at the far end of the carousel removes the shredded Z pinch target and attaches a new one.

Will it work? Scientists and engineers and technicians are working on the project. Perhaps one day you can help humanity find out.

CHAPTER 4

The Way of ITER

Now for something completely different.

Think about passing your finger rapidly through a flame from a match. The heat doesn't burn you because you're not absorbing much of it.

Z heats up to several million degrees, but for only a few billionths of a second. That briefness is one reason that the building that houses Z doesn't burn up. Its firing does wreck steel plates immediately surrounding the wire array. But the temperature in the building stays much the same after a "shot" as before it.

The effects of brief bursts of power have their limits.

But now imagine you want to build a fusion machine containing a plasma of deuterium and tritium ions that *burns not for nanoseconds but for a quarter of an hour* and *at a temperature that far exceeds that of the core of the sun, about 15 million degrees.*

We're not talking solar panels here. We're talking about an effort to create a sun on earth.

At the *ITER* machine, under construction in southern France, the goal is to one day *use the energy from small amounts of continually burning, very hot plasma to make huge amounts of electricity.*

If we could make a plasma that hot, contain it, and extract heat from it, electricity generation would be straightforward. The techniques are known. The heat could be used to turn water (or some other fluid) to steam all day. The steam would turn a wheel that could generate electricity. And only a little bit of matter would be consumed for fuel.

A model of the ITER complex to be completed about 2019. The setting is the countryside of southern France near the research center of Cadarache. (Courtesy ITER)

But heating a plasma to 100 million degrees, and finding a way to contain it, has its challenges.

ITER is the name of the world's first experimental reactor that will be built to heat and maintain a plasma that exceeds 100 million degrees for approximately 15 minutes.

The 10-story machine will have many dramatic qualities.

It will not only house a plasma six times hotter than the sun but cool surrounding components to four degrees above absolute zero, the temperature at which, according to classical physics, all molecular motion stops!

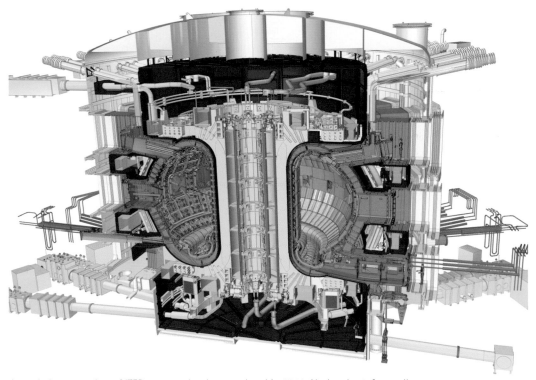

An artist's conception of ITER, expected to be completed in 2019. Notice the 6-foot-tall (2-meters-tall) human in the foreground. (Courtesy ITER)

Absolute zero is a lot colder than what we normally consider zero—the temperature at which ice freezes in the Celsius system. (That's the same as 32 degrees Fahrenheit.) There's a song about someone accused of being "as cold as ice," so that's pretty bad. But absolute zero is the cold of outer space. That's minus 273 degrees C, or minus 459 degrees F, where atoms no longer move. Motion makes heat. No motion, no heat. Absolute zero.

How does steam turn a wheel? Water in a pot becomes steam as its temperature reaches 212 degrees Fahrenheit (100 degrees Celsius), only a little more than twice as hot as the human body. Put a lid on the pot and keep heating. The steam remains steam, but its *molecules* fly around faster, with more energy, creating more pressure.

Think of these molecules as people locked in a room and getting more and more desperate to get out. They pound harder and harder on any doors or windows.

So let's imagine one wall is movable. It's hinged at its top but can swing out from the bottom. The steam pushes the door up and out so the steam can escape, reducing the pressure in the room.

But now imagine the movable wall, instead of hinged to the ceiling, is attached to the surface of an exterior wheel, like one paddle on a paddle wheel. Steam pressure forces the first paddle upward, turning the wheel. The next paddle comes into play as the first one leaves, blocking the steam's release again. If more water is constantly being fed into the pot, turning into steam, the paddle wheel will be kept turning by the steam trying to escape. The steam is doing work.

The escaping steam can be captured, reheated, and used again. And the cycle continues.

But how does steam turning a paddle wheel make electricity?

Remember that every traveling electric current creates a magnetic field around it. Does that work in reverse? Can a moving magnet produce an electric current in a wire?

It could.

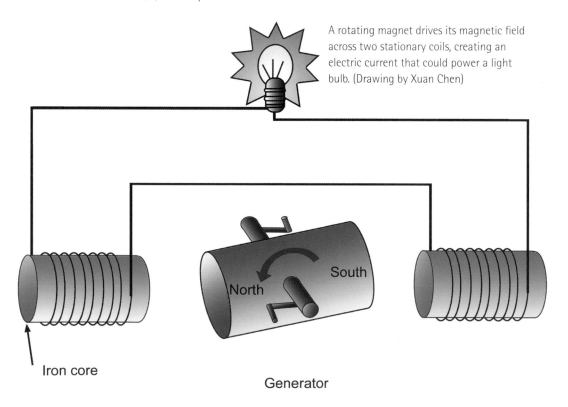

A rotating magnet drives its magnetic field across two stationary coils, creating an electric current that could power a light bulb. (Drawing by Xuan Chen)

Iron core

Generator

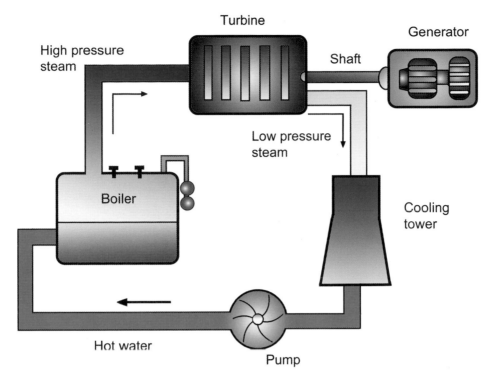

Take a few moments to follow this drawing along. The boiler turns water to steam, which turns the turbine—the modern equivalent of a paddle wheel. The wheel turns a shaft that turns a generator to create electric current. The unused steam is cooled back down to hot water, and the cycle begins again. (Drawing by Xuan Chen)

It may seem odd that what we earlier said was cause and effect can be reversed. An electric current is surrounded by a magnetic field, just like it's supposed to be. It's just that the magnetic field could have generated the electricity instead of the other way around.

Suppose you attached a permanent magnet shaped like a cylinder to the end of the axle turned by the paddle wheels. The magnet then rotates in place. Now place two cylinders of iron, one above and the other below the magnet.

We know that magnets attract iron, yes? Actually, they induce magnetic fields in the iron they attract. Rotate the permanent magnet and you'll find it's easier to turn in some positions than in others. The magnetic fields induced

in the iron pieces above and below swell or decrease in response to the position of the turning magnet.

If you coil wires around the two stationary pieces of iron, that swelling and shrinking magnetic output, called magnetic flux, induces a traveling electric current in the wires, just as a traveling electric current creates a magnetic field around it. If the wires are thick enough, and coiled around the iron cores enough times, and the magnetic field is strong enough, a powerfully propelled paddle wheel could create enough electricity—powerfully shifting magnetic field lines across thick wires—to light a lightbulb or even neighborhoods.

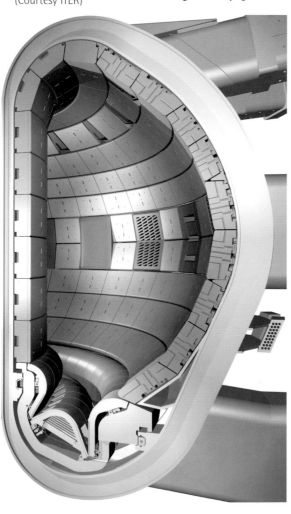

One of those components kept at near absolute zero will be the most powerful magnet ever built on earth.

To keep it so cold, the magnet and related equipment have to be protected against the plasma's enormous heat and its powerful escaping neutrons.

The magnet's first line of physical protection, called a plasma containment wall, will be—strangely—rows of tiles resembling those in a Roman bathhouse of thousands of years ago.

Lithium *blankets* beyond the tiles are expected to capture some of the dangerously powerful neutrons emitted by the plasma. The lithium and neutrons will become tritium, an important part of the fusion process. Tritium then will be fed back into the plasma to make the fusion reaction even hotter and more efficient.

There'll be supercold helium and much, much more.

Want to see the show?

Come on in, it's just starting.

But first, a little history about the name of this machine.

Originally, ITER was an acronym for *international thermonuclear experimental reactor*. But project leaders feared that the words *thermonuclear*, *experimental*, and *reactor* linked in a single phrase could upset the public, as though there could be a nuclear explosion if something went wrong. Would you want a reactor like that in your backyard? Or anywhere close?

Of course, ITER will run on fused atoms, not fissioned ones. It wouldn't explode if things went wrong but only stop working. Still, leaders thought it best to ditch the acronym.

Fortunately for the project, *iter* happens to be a word in Latin. It means "the path" or "the way."

Since its researchers believe that ITER may indeed be "the way" to create nuclear fusion—electricity from seawater—on earth, "the way" is now the formal explanation of the name of this machine.

Perhaps the machine is at least *a* way among others, if it can heat a material roughly six times hotter than the core of the sun and keep it burning on earth. The feat at first seems incredible.

Consider the temperatures at which we normally cook things.

We burn wood at a campfire. Most wood burns at only 300 to 400 degrees F (150 to 200 degrees C).

We usually use electricity or gas in an oven. Home ovens heat to approximately 500 degrees F (250 C).

Gas and oil in industrial furnaces can reach temperatures of roughly 2,000 degrees F (roughly 1,000 C).

You would have to live a long time before those methods heated any material to more than 100 million degrees C, the temperature at which ITER will operate. Actually, these materials never would.

But even if a plasma could be heated that hot, that long, what material on earth could contain it? That plasma is more than six times hotter than the core of the sun, generally thought to be about 15 million degrees.

The answer is: no material on earth could contain it.

Isn't it alarming to imagine a plasma of more than 100 million degrees roaming the countryside? Out of control?

So let's talk first about how we'd control this plasmoid creature if we could create it, and we'll sidle into how to house and heat it as we go.

Matter can't be used to contain plasma that hot. But magnetic fields could do the trick. Those fields are energy, not material. They might waver or not be strong enough or just wink out, but they don't burn.

We've already learned the important role magnetic fields play at Z. Scientists think that magnetic fields, generated at the proper intensity, could do the job at ITER.

But these magnetic fields won't originate naturally out of the fusion-producing process, as they do at Z. ITER's powerful magnetic fields must be deliberately created. It's no small task. It will require construction of the most powerful magnet ever made on earth.

Containing ITER plasma by magnetic fields: scientists intend plasma to race around the donut-shaped space in the diagram. But how to keep material six times hotter than the sun contained there? Remember that magnetic fields are generated at right angles to the movement of electric current. See if you can find the fields that humans think can control the hot ionized gas that forms the plasma. (Drawing by Xuan Chen)

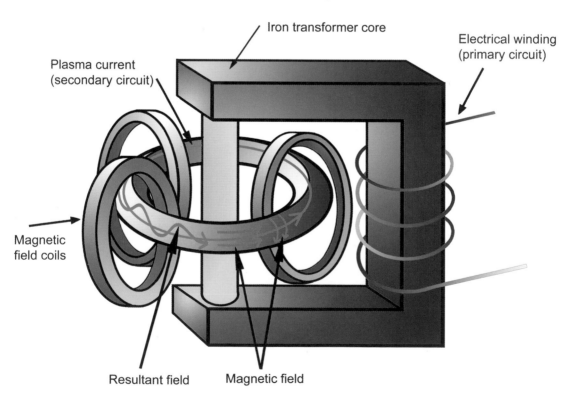

How strong? Well, earth's north-south magnetic field (which birds may follow when they migrate) averages about half a *gauss*. (A gauss is a unit of magnetic field strength.)

Magnetic resonance imaging (MRI) machines are the big cylinders into whose empty cores doctors slide you to look inside your body. These usually function at 15,000 gauss (15 kilogauss), magnetizing and aligning the water molecules in your body for picture taking.

Probably the closest in strength to the ITER magnet is at CERN, a European laboratory at the very forefront of high-energy physics. That machine can blast streams of high-energy protons into each other. CERN's magnet strength is 40,000 gauss (40 kilogauss).

ITER's main magnetic field strength will be roughly 100 thousand gauss (100 kilogauss).

So the ITER magnet will be 200,000 times stronger than earth's average magnetic field, more than six times stronger than a typical MRI, and more than twice as strong as the magnet at CERN. That is how strong scientists estimate the main magnetic field must be to restrain the fusion plasma expected to be burning at ITER.

The magnetic field generated by Sandia Laboratories' Z machine is far more powerful than that created at ITER. Z magnetic field reaches approximately 40 million gauss, far stronger than ITER's ongoing magnetic field of 100 thousand gauss. But they have different applications and *parameters*.

Z's field compresses plasma over a tiny volume—about 0.1 cubic inch (one cubic centimeter). It does this for less than 100 nanoseconds. It powerfully squeezes ions together to release x-rays that produce fusion.

ITER's magnetic field will stay on for a comparative eternity—15 minutes. It controls (but does not tightly squeeze) 1,134 cubic yards (840 cubic meters) of plasma in a container that resembles a giant donut. The donut, called a torus, is 20.3 feet (6.2 meters) along its long axis and 6.7 feet (two meters) along its short axis.

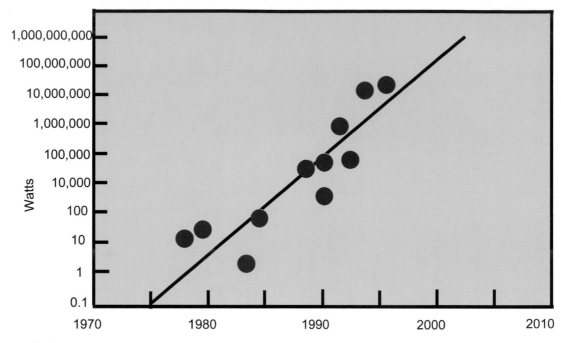

Fusion power is sometimes dismissed as an impossible dream. But, as the graph shows, the ability of experimental magnetic fusion devices to generate power has increased a million times over twenty years, rivaling the rate of improvements of computer chips. (Data from informational brochure "Fusion Science" from General Atomics)

In a way, a magnetic field around a plasma functions like a plastic curtain stopping shower water from spraying a bathroom. A plasma's energized isotopes are moving very rapidly because that's what a plasma's particles do when they get hot. The wraparound magnetic field keeps most of the charged-particle plasma contained within the shower stall, turning back those trying to leave. Magnetic fields will confine most charged particles to one area.

To achieve such strong magnetic fields, *superconducting materials* will be used that don't resist the flow of electricity when a current passes through them. This allows large, continuing electrical currents to create large, continuing magnetic fields needed to contain the plasma.

Electrical energy meeting resistance in a wire is changed in part into heat energy. This lost electrical energy can't be used to create magnetic fields. It's also a major cause of power loss in electricity's trip from distant electrical generators to your home. Hence, scientists have sought materials that could conduct electricity with less loss to heat. They wanted a superconducting material.

Fortunately, some compounds of materials discovered in the last few decades, if cooled to nearly absolute zero, conduct electricity with extremely little resistance. So almost no electricity passing through them is converted to heat.

Because of the low heat losses, once electricity begins traveling through these materials, it just keeps traveling. Compared with the transmission of ordinary electricity, this behavior seems either marvelous or spooky, depending on your state of mind. But it means that almost no electricity after the initial large start-up input is needed to maintain the electric current in a superconducting material. It just keeps traveling through. So the enormous magnetic field it naturally creates exists as long as the electric current.

So superconducting materials were the obvious choice for the giant ITER magnets.

But Nature doesn't let us off the hook so easily. Very large amounts of power are needed to power the refrigeration unit that cools liquid helium to four degrees above absolute zero. The liquid helium is pumped through pipes interspersed among strands and coils of magnets, keeping them cold despite the enormous heat from the plasma.

ITER (or a bigger successor based on the ITER model) is expected to maintain its own refrigeration from the electric power the plasma ultimately will generate.

Cooling its own magnets and other components will be a drain on ITER's (or its successor's) output, but there should still be plenty of electricity left over for other purposes.

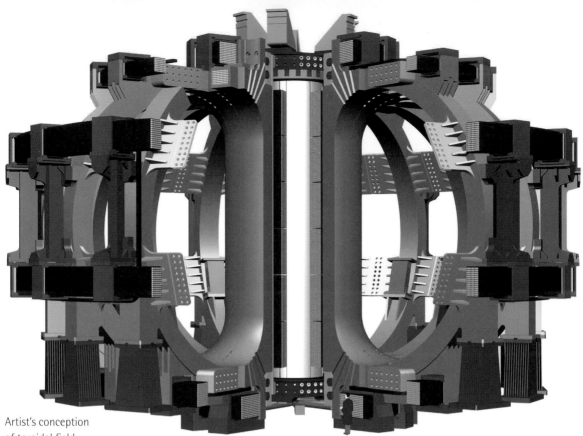

Artist's conception of toroidal field coils. The word *toroidal* looks complicated but only means it surrounds the torus, or donut-shape, in which the plasma is contained. Imagine electricity passing around the kidney-shaped structures, creating magnetic fields to help keep the plasma within. It's a little like cowboys on horseback, on the outside of a herd of cattle, pushing to keep them together, isn't it? (Courtesy ITER)

Now imagine the space needed to contain the plasma. Its ions and electrons must be housed so they don't just rush off into the rest of the machine. Runaway ions lower the temperature of the plasma when they cut class and leave. That's not good. And there's the additional expense of sending new hydrogen ions into the collision chamber to make up for ones that ran off.

Ions confined and at high temperatures have the greatest chance of colliding and fusing. We want that.

An effective method scientists have found to encourage these charged ions to stick around is to send them around and around a kind of three-dimensional race track set up in the shape of a donut. The technical term for this donut is a *torus*. The idea for this was first developed in the 1960s by scientists in the former Soviet Union. It was called a *tokomak*.

No mass murderer was ever confined with more caution in jail than plasma in this torus. Superconducting electrical cables forming superconducting magnets will be coiled around the torus like many vertical rings on a rounded index finger held horizontal. Electrical wires also travel lengthwise around the torus (that is, around the horizontally bent finger). A vertical magnetic source called a solenoid goes up the center of the torus in the z direction (through the vacancy in the center of the bent finger). These electrically charged, superconducting metals will create magnetic fields in intersecting planes that keep the plasma within the torus. They will gently rebuff charged particles trying to escape by bending the paths of their flight so that they stay within the area.

But you can imagine that to trap superheated ions like this for a long time isn't easy. Such plasmas generate a condition known as *turbulence*. This is like the confusing movement of air molecules in a hurricane. The molecules' paths are so complicated that the best computers can't completely define them.

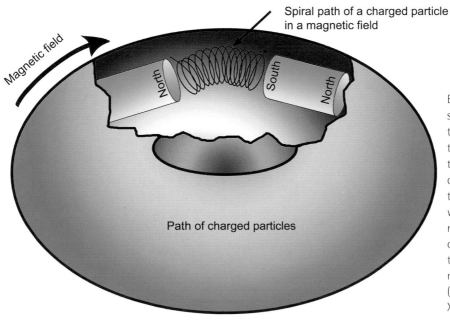

Spiral path of a charged particle in a magnetic field

Magnetic field

North

South

North

Path of charged particles

Basic magnetic confinement (Tokamak design)

Because the ions spiral as they travel along their path, few touch the walls of the torus. If they did, the gas would lose heat, making the job of reaching high temperatures more difficult. (Drawing by Xuan Chen)

Keeping a magnetically confined plasma burning is a little like maintaining a person on life support.

Both have to be fed. The human may have to be fed intravenously to make energy to live. Because the plasma has no mouth, its food too must be somehow injected into it. More heated hydrogen isotopes—yum!—must be added to keep up its strength.

Both generate waste products that must be removed, because leaving them there is so unhealthy that it could kill the organisms. Human waste can be toxic. Ash from a fusion fire—active ions that have become passive atoms and block fusion processes rather than create them—need to be removed through a channel called a *divertor* so their buildup doesn't smother the reaction.

The temperature of both human and plasma must be monitored and maintained; if their temperatures drop too low, both plasma and human will die.

Human patients can die from bed sores. The plasma's skin—the magnetic fields that keep it together—needs constant attention so that it too doesn't develop sores. The plasma equivalent of bed sores occurs when instabilities take over, rupturing what should be the smooth shape of a plasma and causing its death.

Here's the difference. Keeping a human alive in that state may be a good thing morally, yet it may not produce immediate benefits to society.

But if you can feed, house, and clean a plasma while keeping it warm enough to survive and preventing turbulence from distorting it, you could have created the most unimaginable energy source humans have ever known: a small pet sun on earth.

The difficulties created by turbulence are one reason why the lives of magnetically confined, very hot plasmas have been brief, on the order of a few seconds or less. Turbulence creates instabilities in plasmas, shutting them down.

Inertial confinement machines like Z deal with this problem by maintaining a plasma for only nanoseconds, and even then plasma kinks are a problem. ITER will attempt to maintain its plasma for 15 minutes. It's not yet clear how the magnetic fields should be set up to avoid plasma instabilities. This will be one of the tests of the ITER machine. Some scientists believe that the bigger and more powerful the machine, the more controllable the plasma.

So now we finally arrive at the question: how do you heat a plasma that hot?

The answer is: with great difficulty.

A plasma can be heated in several ways.

Because a plasma's free electrons (remember that a plasma is composed of ions and electrons) will carry current, electricity can be sent through the plasma to heat it. The remainder of the plasma will resist the passage of electricity. This raises the plasma's temperature, just as an ordinary wire gets warm or even melts when a large amount of electricity is passed through it (as happens in the Z wire array).

That's pretty simple.

But Nature isn't so easily figured out. As the plasma's temperature rises, its ions become so energetic that they won't let the current through. The electric current stops increasing the plasma's temperature in the 20- to 30-million-degree range. In other words, this heating method will only take us so far. In nuclear fusion terms, that's hardly even a hot day at the beach. Everybody, off the bus. We need to find a different vehicle for further heat transport.

We want to add energy to the plasma to make it hotter. Fortunately, another method exists that can pick up the pace. It involves sending a beam of high-energy atoms (not ions) into the plasma.

Scientists follow this cookbook approach: send a gas of deuterium ions toward a porous grid electrically charged to a high voltage. The high voltage pulls the ions forward and speeds them up. Now sprinkle these sped-up ions into a gas of ordinary neutral deuterium atoms. The ions have more energy and more attractive power than the sleepy atoms at rest. So the energized ions strip electrons from the atoms. The highly energetic ions are now highly energetic atoms. They are also—very important to getting through a magnetic field—electrically neutral.

Now take the highly energized but electrically neutral deuterium atoms and beam them into the plasma. Because the beam is neutral, it can pass through the guardian magnetic field and enter the plasma without being deflected away. But once in, these unsuspecting high-steppers are immediately mugged by the plasma, stripped of their electrons, and turned loose as more high-energy ions. These transfer energy into other ions when they collide with them. Like a drunken person staggering through a room, they will have numerous interactions. The energy they bring to the plasma raises its temperature.

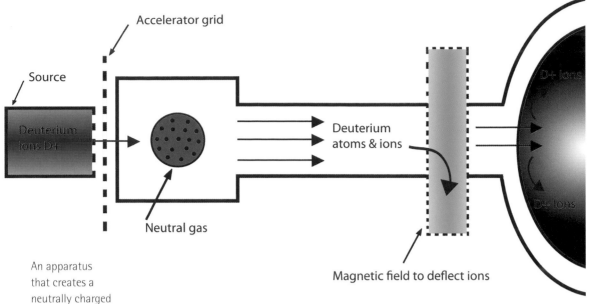

Accelerator grid

Source

Deuterium
ions D+

Neutral gas

Deuterium
atoms & ions

Magnetic field to deflect ions

D+ ions

D+ ions

An apparatus that creates a neutrally charged beam—that is, a beam with no charge—to heat plasma. The ions are accelerated and then changed into high-energy atoms. Atoms have no electric charge, so they then can enter the plasma without deflection by the watchdog magnetic beams. (Drawing by Xuan Chen)

A third possible method is magnetic compression, used to great effect at Z. Any compression increases the temperature of the plasma (the same energy in a smaller space means greater heat per unit area), thereby increasing the speed with which its components zip around. This increases the temperature of the plasma. The smaller space also brings ions closer together. Both increased speed and greater proximity increase the likelihood of impact.

A further option: a generator broadcasting energy at frequencies appropriate to plasma particles can heat them. Can't imagine this? Think about a radio station sending out music at frequencies to which your radio responds. How about an oven radiating microwaves, making food hot? In this case, the broadcast energy is keyed to exactly that best absorbed by deuterium and tritium.

Did I say tritium? The most effective combination to produce nuclear fusion on earth at this time is the interaction of deuterium and tritium ions. Deuterium is readily available from seawater. But tritium is short lived and hard to find.

Fortunately, the cheap and widely available element lithium may surround the reaction like a blanket. When lithium is struck by neutrons emerging from the plasma, it converts into a tritium gas, which is fed back into the reaction. This is called a *breeder reaction*.

But not every neutron is captured. Like bullets fired up into the air, some can come down where you don't want them and cause damage. So the surfaces of the magnets have to be protected by shielding not only against the heat of the plasma but against scoring of their surfaces by very energetic neutrons emitted by the reaction.

And there are other emissions, like x-rays and alpha particles, that result from the fusion process and must be dealt with.

Darth Vader's sunglasses? Well, shades of a kind. The proposed blanket module is intended to shield the superconducting magnets and other equipment from the heat and neutrons generated by the fusion reaction. It may also be used to "breed" tritium. (Courtesy ITER)

Then there is the equivalent of ash from the fusion fire that must be disposed of. Some deuterium and tritium ions drift to the outer edge of the donut as they circle. They may capture less energetic electrons and become atoms. Atoms don't fuse. These must be removed from the main plasma through a divertor so that they don't build up in number and cool the reaction.

So . . . what do we have? A superconducting magnet to be cooled almost to absolute zero and the plasma its magnetic fields will contain to be six times hotter than the sun.

That's quite a trick, to have something that cold a few feet from something that hot. It's like putting a hot, hot oven in your cold, cold freezer. Something's gotta give, right? The freezer's trying to stay cold. The oven's trying to stay hot. Can this couple survive?

The answer is yes, but it takes planning.

To sum up: The purpose of the ITER project is to show that humans can use magnetic fields to safely and effectively contain gases burning hotter than the sun for a quarter hour at a stretch.

And that the burning plasma can be kept stable, like a gas flame on a stove top, not collapsing here or flaring there or winking out totally.

And that a liquid helium bath can keep the magnets cool.

And that superconducting materials can be used for the magnets.

And that a "blanket" made of lithium can be created to absorb deadly, destructive neutrons and turn them into tritium, which can be sent back into the plasma to strengthen the fusion reaction.

And that water or some other fluid passing in pipes through the moderated heat from the plasma can be turned into steam and power a generator.

A cooling test module delivered to a site in Japan in November 1998. Work to perfect techniques to be used at ITER has been going on for a long time. (Courtesy ITER)

These difficulties and more are why magnetic fusion has been achieved in only a few labs around the world, and so far very briefly. Just enough to make scientists think it can be done longer to greater purpose.

Diagrams of the machine are so flowing and complicated, strange parts melting into each other, that ITER looks like comic book drawings of the machine of the future.

But it's no comic book, and magnetic confinement could help save the earth if it works.

Turn the page.

CHAPTER 5

Problems of the Way

You know how simply an i-Phone works? Very cool. Not only does it take pictures, but you can bring them up close by opening your fingers on the viewing screen. You can get a wider, more distant view by closing your fingers on the screen. No need to find, push, or turn stupid levers or buttons or knobs.

But making that phone work so simply wasn't easy. It took a lot of thinking that's just not visible. It's the same way that good actors put in effort offstage to make playing a role onstage look easy. Months of work are behind a performance that looks so natural. The same with rock bands—long rehearsals in the garage create that seamless outpouring of music.

It's like that with ITER. It has to be a model for a super-smooth generating plant that will produce electricity seamlessly and with little apparent effort. Here are a few of the problems engineers and scientists will have to overcome to make ITER a reality—to keep alive a burning fusion plasma so that it looks like no problem at all.

We've said that ITER's plasma has to be hotter than the sun to fuse atoms. This extra heat is needed because ITER won't have the sun's immense gravity to help pull atoms together. The sun's gravity produces pressures estimated at about 400 billion times the earth's atmospheric pressure at sea level. This gravitational force corrals ions and compresses plasmas that would otherwise escape. We

Two positive
charges repel each
other, right? Go
into a store that
sells magnets
and try to bring
together the same
charged ends of
two magnets. Bet
you can't do it.

don't know how to reproduce a gravitational field that strong on earth. So our plasmas must be heated hotter so that their ions and electrons career more madly than the sun's. This increased velocity raises the chance that the ions will overcome their reluctance to meet.

Given the increased heat and accompanying speed of movement in the ITER machine, enough ions are expected to strike each other to create fusion.

But not necessarily reach *ignition*—the condition where the plasma becomes hot enough to burn by itself. Cutbacks in funding meant that a smaller ITER had to be built than originally proposed, powered by 15 mega-amperes rather than the 20 mega-amps that scientists believe necessary to commence a high-yield burn that would sustain itself. So external heat will have to be applied to keep the reaction hot enough for fusion reactions to occur.

That's with today's technology. The machine will still be useful in understanding the conditions for fusion, and it's possible that over the intervening years till its estimated start-up date around 2019, more effective tools to generate fusion might make the 15 mega-amps enough.

Buuut . . . we still need to contain the plasma. And remember, we want this fusion cloud to be . . . smooth. Like the sun. Stable. The sun's gravity pulls its gases into the most economical shape: a sphere. We'll settle for less, but whatever the shape, we want stability. But that doesn't happen easily in nature. Under magnetic control, the plasma may twist like a snake or tie itself into knots like a balloon tied off in several places along its length. Then it winks out. How can we make this plasma stable?

It's like trying to sit on a ball partially filled with air or water—the slightest change in the way you're sitting and the thing beneath you squishes out in a new way. You get a kind of ripple where too many atoms are in one place and it's, say, hot here and not hot enough there and the whole reaction shuts down like a snuffed match. How do you avoid instabilities?

In Z, the plasma's life is very brief, limiting the time that instabilities have to grow. ITER intends to hold a plasma together for a relatively long time. That's tricky.

Then again, how do you cool a machine that hot? Like a radiator system cools a car (but with a lot more complications), frozen helium keeps temperatures down and water can usefully remove heat deposited when alpha particles and neutrons smash into shielding walls. Beryllium tiles and lithium blankets, all contained within a vacuum inside a steel frame, play defense for the magnetic coils. These sit farthest removed from the plasma.

Clearly, first-class pumps and a top-flight cooling system are needed to keep ITER cool.

But a large number of other details are essential to success. To give an idea of the complexity, here are a few of them:

The complete ITER will require a storage tank for hydrogen to replenish what escapes from the burning plasma and a channel through which to send in the isotopes that will continually replenish the plasma.

Did I mention earlier the word *radioactive*? I did. That means you don't want to be inside that machine to make repairs, and neither does anyone else.

In science-fiction movies, people sometimes dress up in special suits that are supposed to stop radioactivity. People wear such suits on space walks around the space station. But some radioactive emissions can't be stopped by a suit light enough for a human to walk in. To block strong radiation requires a block of lead or some other heavy material sitting there like a wall for shielding.

So if something goes wrong inside the machine—and something eventually goes wrong inside any machine—it will need to be remotely handled by a person in a control room remotely operating robots that remove damaged parts. The robot would have to take the part to a "hot cell"—a room where radioactive parts can be taken and refurbished without endangering people—and then returned. Researchers estimate it could take two months—two months!—to find and replace a small part in the most difficult places.

A major repair could take six months.

What else? There's got to be a mechanism to inject fuel into the plasma and ports to exhaust spent fuel gases, just like in a car's engine. There must be a way to clean it of waste material—ash—produced by the burning reaction so it can continue unchoked by spent fuel, just like any other fire.

There must be tools and tanks to collect and process any contamination from leaks throughout the plant. Fuel sources can be reinjected. Impurities can be stored for disposal.

Of course, a control system linking diagnostics—the sensors and computer programs that can find and analyze problems—to the data-logging system that records these events is a must. Basic gases like compressed air for cleaning parts and nitrogen for supercooling are important, as are liquids for firefighting and sanitation, monitors for radiation, and sampling systems (including radiation monitors) throughout the machine to stay on top of problems before they develop big-time.

Simple, huh?

But ITER isn't starting from scratch. The nations of the world didn't decide to invest $14 billion in this project just on a whim. This method has enjoyed worldwide interest from scientists. Smaller prototype devices have been built over several decades. They have showed promise at cooler temperatures and for seconds of time in the United

States, Russia, China, Australia, and Great Britain, and at a number of sites in Europe. The idea at ITER is to see if researchers can get it to run for a quarter hour or so, producing megawatts of fusion power over a longer period. That will show the method works.

We now have enough knowledge that an overview of ITER and the times it lives in might be helpful.

ITER is the most expensive of the attempts to devise a method to create electricity from seawater. Its $14 billion funding makes it roughly 140 times the expense of renovating Sandia's Z machine ($90 million) and more than four times as expensive as a laser machine we come to next: the National Ignition Facility in California, currently funded at a little over $3 billion.

It's taken 12 years just to design the ITER machine. Why does it take so long? Why is an actual power plant based on its principles expected to begin construction in Japan (rather than anywhere else) sometime in the early 2030s, once the ITER machine proves out successful by 2019? Why is nuclear fusion always 30 years away, as critics sometimes say?

The reasons for delays and location changes sometimes seem more about politics than science. National pride, as well as national purse strings, is involved. Changes in locations and delays in fusion funding have helped retard nuclear fusion's development, like a child getting too little food can be slow to develop.

Complicated issues are involved. A nation has money, and then its economy tanks and it doesn't. It's interested, and then it's not. And then maybe it is again.

Does this remind you of anything? Sometimes, nations seem to act like kids in school. Nations may have flags and patriotic songs, do wonderful things like traveling to the moon, or be responsible for saving people's lives, but the strange thing is, in a way, looked at from a distance, they act like kids do. They're friends, and then they're not friends, and then maybe they're friends again. They support each other for a while, and then they don't. They're in; they're out. Scientists like to describe the reasons for human behavior in terms of neurons firing in the brain. In nations, they call it politics. But it may come to the same thing.

The United States was part of the project. Then it decided to drop out. Now it's back in. Canada was in; now it's out. India was out; now it's in. Currently, seven participants form the "in" group. These are the European Union, Japan, the United States, Russia, India, China, and South Korea. But just as more kids want to join a group when it gets status, more countries are thinking of joining ITER as it moves forward. Maybe they want the prestige. Maybe they want to help the human race. Maybe they want firsthand experience in helping build what may be the power plants of the future. Among the latest potential members are Brazil and Kazakhstan.

In a way, it's a wonderful thing to have the nations of earth join in a peaceful project. No nation has a monopoly on ideas. Every country has a different outlook. That diversity of viewpoints can bring new ideas that will help make the project better.

Of course they also speak different languages. They have different safety regulations. They have different measurement units. The threads on screws may be a different pitch. Wall currents of electricity use different voltages. Even standards of politeness and what is acceptable behavior are different. And time zones are different, so one scientist may be sleeping when another wants to talk with him or her. (Siberia, for example, is 13 hours ahead of New Mexico, so finding joint working hours can be a problem.) And there's always the possibility that a country is proposing some task or change for its own benefit—to make it more important or bring more money to its shores—not the group's. So working together is a challenge.

Yet if funding and science go forward, almost before we know it, Japan will be building the world's first fusion power plant. Everyone involved hopes to actually produce useful electricity from the method.

By that time, you'll be in college or graduate school. Prepare now. They'll need you.

The dream of laser beams and the unusual power of their light has excited the imagination of humans for decades. Not surprising, then, to learn that a service cart at the NIF facility bears the name *Enterprise*, the name of the imaginary starship of the fanciful *Star Trek* space-based federation. This laser bay transporter is an automated guided vehicle used to help transport and install laser parts. (Courtesy Lawrence Livermore National Laboratory and National Security, LLC, and the US Department of Energy)

CHAPTER 6

The Stunning Lasers of NIF

The *National Ignition Facility*, usually referred to as NIF, expects to reach fusion through use of super-powerful lasers. The project, at Lawrence Livermore National Laboratory in Livermore, California, is proud to acknowledge its resemblance to the futuristic television show *Star Trek*.

A service cart that traverses the facility, in fact, bears the label *Enterprise*, the name of the spaceship used by several generations of Federation captains.

An explanation put out by the facility titled "How NIF Works" opens with the famous *Star Trek* phrase, "Beam me up." The difference, though, between the TV show and NIF: When spaceship *Enterprise* crew members ran into dangerous situations, they were usually instructed to set their handheld lasers on "stun."

At NIF, they're set on "burn."

NIF was originally conceived to provide data for supercomputer simulations by using the most powerful lasers on earth to heat materials to extremely high temperatures and pressures. When achieved, such results will enable scientists to better explore the conditions in nuclear weapons and the interior of suns.

But NIF also could become the method of choice in the struggle to produce energy from nuclear fusion, a carbon-free source.

The sphere hangs there in space, with machined ports staring out in every direction. Death star? No, too colorful.

The ports, on second look, resemble craters, lots of them. Model of the moon hanging above the earth?

Actually, the portals are entry holes for 192 laser beams so arranged that they will simultaneously blast, from many angles, a tiny target capsule at the center of the 33-foot-diameter (10-meter-diameter), one-million-pound (2.2-million-kilogram) sphere. The idea is to fuse the deuterium and tritium frozen within the capsule.

Housed in a facility the size of three football fields, the lasers will put all their radiated power into a target the size of a BB.

That radiated power will equal 500 trillion watts—about 1,000 times the electric power generated in the United States—and create

NIF's target chamber being hoisted into place. (Courtesy Lawrence Livermore National Laboratory and National Security, LLC, and the US Department of Energy)

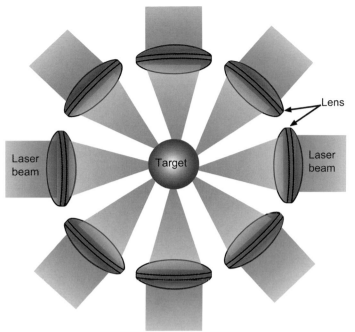

This simplified drawing shows how laser beams will attempt to compress NIF's tiny fusion capsule. In reality, there will be 192 beams, striking the pellet directly or heating its container (a little can called a hohlraum that acts as an oven). The lasers will beam from all three dimensions, rather than on the x-y plane of the drawing. (Drawing by Xuan Chen)

pressures on the capsule that exceed 100 billion times the earth's atmosphere.

True, the power burst only lasts for nanoseconds. For so brief a time, even that colossal amount of power won't light up anyone's city block. But it wouldn't be wise to put your hand at the focal point of the lasers of the National Ignition Facility.

The NIF building will house 192 lasers.

Each, by itself, is more powerful than any laser in the world.

When those lasers flash on at the same time, their tiny target will be

The site: the lasers and target area are the size of three football fields. (Courtesy Lawrence Livermore National Laboratory and National Security, LLC, and the US Department of Energy)

Laser bay 2, one of NIF's two light "factories" where light is amplified from hardly visible beginnings into the most powerful beam of light in the world. (Courtesy Lawrence Livermore National Laboratory and National Security, LLC, and the US Department of Energy)

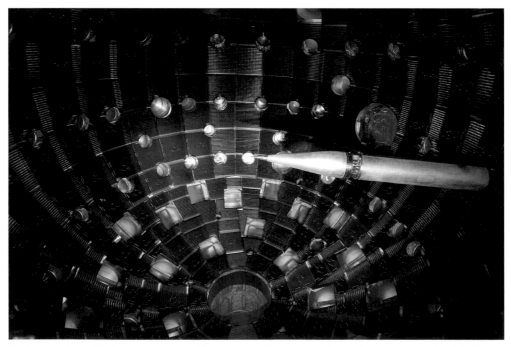

An interior view of NIF's target chamber. The target positioner, which holds the target, is on the right. The target must be aligned more precisely than the thickness of a human hair. (Courtesy Lawrence Livermore National Laboratory and National Security, LLC, and the US Department of Energy)

heated far hotter than the sun—more than 100 million degrees—and near instantly . . . disappear!

But not before—hopefully—the deuterium and tritium ions at the center of the capsule fuse, releasing neutrons that drive the remaining isotopes in the capsule to fusion.

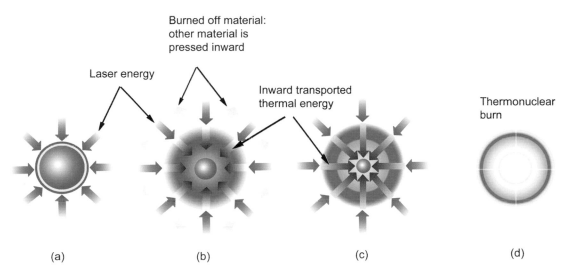

Laser energy directed at a capsule (fig. a) burns off material (fig. b). In an equal and opposite reaction, like two cue balls striking each other, the departing material like rocket exhaust pushes the remaining material inward (fig. c) until fusion results (fig. d). (Drawing by Xuan Chen)

Perhaps you recognize that the method of NIF is closer to that of the Z machine than to that of ITER. Like Z, NIF will use a nanosecond pulse of power to compress a tiny capsule to create fusion rather than maintain an ongoing cloud of fusion gas for minutes like ITER. NIF will use laser beams for compression instead of magnetism and ions, as does Z. But both NIF and Z use the fusion method known as inertial confinement rather than the magnetic confinement used by ITER. (You might glance back at the discussion in chapter 2 if you've forgotten these terms.)

How do you get a hugely powerful beam of light?

At NIF, you start small, with a beam of infrared light so weak that even standing in a darkened room with infrared goggles, you could barely see it.

It's powered by only a billionth of a watt.

Energy is added to the beam as it passes on its way.

Just as, augmented by feeder streams, a trickle of water in the mountains eventually becomes a major river, additions to NIF's initial trickle of light will turn it into a torrent.

But instead of taking hours or days, NIF's buildup happens in 25 billionths of a second.

It begins by passing the weak initial laser light through glass slabs.

This nearly 800-pound synthetic crystal, grown for NIF, was sliced into 40-cm (15.8-inch) thick plates to focus, transmit, and direct laser beams on their way to the target chamber. (Courtesy Lawrence Livermore National Laboratory and National Security, LLC, and the US Department of Energy)

The slabs are altered—the preferred term is *doped*—by a material called *neodymium* that is made part of the glass. There are a lot of neodymium atoms in this system: 10^{23}, or 10 with 23 zeros after it. These atoms are important because, when stimulated, they release light only at the *frequency* of the laser beam. (The beam itself is also generated from neodymium-doped material.)

Adjacent to the doped glass slabs, flashlamps powered by powerful capacitors go off brightly and suddenly, like flashbulbs. Flashlamp output looks to the human eye like white light, although its frequencies range from the ultraviolet to the infrared. Only a small part of that light—in the infrared range—is absorbed by the neodymium atoms.

The absorbed energy pushes the neodymium electrons on the slabs into an excited, or stimulated, state. The electrons are uncomfortable in that state, like a person who's eaten too much food. The electrons want to vomit out the excess energy and return to their normal state. The weak beam passing through the glass slab acts as the emetic. The neodymium hurls its excess energy into the initial beam. The beam gets stronger.

Despite the best efforts of scientists, this process is not yet very efficient. While flashlamps are roughly 75 percent efficient in converting electricity from the capacitors into flash light, only 5 percent of that 75 percent is at the right *wavelength* to be stored by the neodymium. Much of the energy, then, is unused and turns into heat, which must be dissipated before the laser can fire again.

But there are a lot of flashlamps (7,680 of them, set in 3,072 glass slabs). Their outputs add to the beam's strength, just like many rivulets coming down a mountain add to a river.

The laser beam, as it picks up power, is energized further by being reflected back and forth four times through the energized area by mirrors rather than simply proceeding down the mountain like the stream of water.

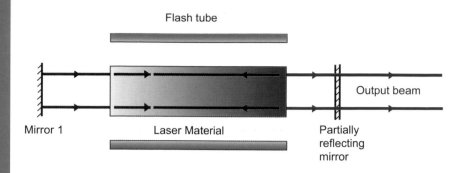

Flash tube

Output beam

Mirror 1   Laser Material   Partially reflecting mirror

The word *laser* is an acronym. That means each of its letters stands for a word. *Laser* really should be written in capital letters—LASER—but over time, *laser* became a word on its own. Let's figure it out. We can stimulate some substance, like a ruby, into giving up light, which is a form of radiation. If we put mirrors on either side of the ruby, we can get the reflected emitted light to pass through the ruby again and stimulate the emission of more light, amplifying the beam. So, logically enough, *laser* stands for *l*ight *a*mplified by the *s*timulated *e*mission of *r*adiation.

The laser light moves so fast, crisscrossing the amplifying area in 100 nanoseconds, that the flashlamp-emitted light, emitted in 300 microseconds, is still present to energize more of the laser light on its back-and-forth travel.

Three hundred microseconds, after all, is 300,000 nanoseconds! To the 100-nanosecond laser light, the flashlamp light seems to be there forever. Similarly, we humans experience the geologic world around us as permanent because our lives are so very brief and geologic time so long.

The mirrors are specially coated to best reflect the wavelength of the light beams. The mirrors also must be very stable so they don't vibrate and unintentionally distort the beam or change its direction even a little.

Close attention is paid to the angles at which light passes through glass to minimize the loss of energy to unwanted reflection. (When you look in a store window and see a dim reflection of yourself, it means not all the light is going through the window. Some is being reflected back at you. That's not wanted here.)

A lot of equipment is there to groom the beam, just as you yourself get groomed in a barbershop or hair salon.

The entering light is turned at different angles (*polarized*) so that it can absorb more energy.

A *deformable mirror* contorts itself to correct any deformities in the light beam and remove the blemishes. The light emerges smooth and clear.

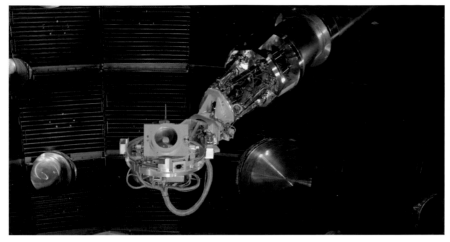

Groomer: this machine analyzes the quality of the beams arriving at the firing chamber. (Courtesy Lawrence Livermore National Laboratory and National Security, LLC, and the US Department of Energy)

Researchers work to eliminate hot (bright) spots in the beam to make its power uniform.

That goes for dark (cold) spots: researchers don't want them.

Scientists also want to make sure the outside corners of the square-shaped laser beams are as energized as their hot centers.

And they want to make sure that all parts of the front of the wave are traveling through space at exactly the same time so that some parts don't arrive slightly in front of the other.

Why would anyone want a deformable mirror? To correct for tiny beam distortions, like a good haircut correcting a bad one. There are 39 (count them; I did) manipulators that slightly change the shape of the mirror on the other side. (Courtesy Lawrence Livermore National Laboratory and National Security, LLC, and the US Department of Energy)

Every part of the light, like music from a band, has to be trained to downbeat at the same time, with the same emphasis, to avoid a ragged performance.

The light beam's passage through a later laser section called the "switchyard" diverges the beams from their compact positioning, one next to another, into lower and upper beams that will eventually separate still further.

The light is no longer a trickle. It is beginning, you might say, to become a torrent.

As the beam is strengthened, it is split into 48 and then 192 laser beams.

The light has traveled a thousand feet before entering the target chamber.

There, it passes through lenses and converges on the *fusion capsule*.

An artist's conception of the energy surrounding a capsule in a NIF hohlraum. Light from the laser enters the hohlraum, which contains energy like an oven. (Courtesy Lawrence Livermore National Laboratory and National Security, LLC, and the US Department of Energy)

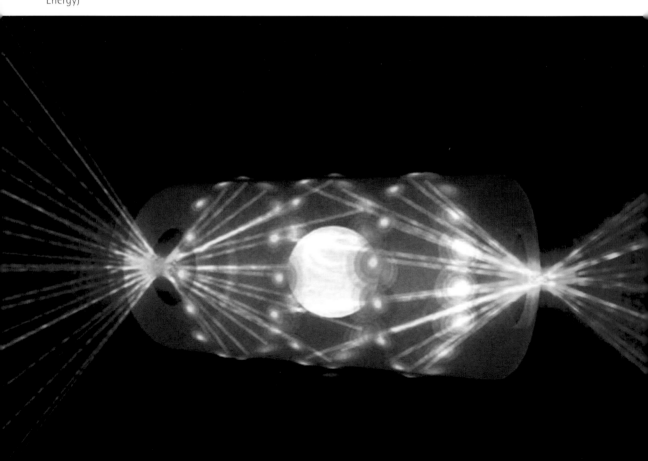

Can you imagine a square beam being focused down to a point? The beams in the firing chamber resemble square inverted pyramids as they attack the tiny capsule of hydrogen isotopes.

NIF's initial weak beam by now has been amplified more than a quadrillion times. It is 10 to the 15th power—10 with 15 zeros after it—stronger than the initial weak beam. It happened faster than you could blink.

The added energy is 99.99 percent of NIF's striking power.

Laser beams are created by annoying some poor substance until it puts out light. Like, for example, a ruby. If you send enough energy into a ruby—stake it out with big floodlamps shining on it—"Confess, ruby! We know where you were on Tuesday night!"—the ruby will "sing," as they called a confession in the 1930s gangster movies. That is, the chromium in the ruby will be stimulated to emit its own radiation. And that radiation will be at the single frequency at which chromium generates light.

The first laser was actually made from exciting a ruby until it emitted light.

At NIF, a rare earth material called neodymium is excited to create an *infrared* beam.

What are wavelengths and frequencies? They can be imagined in terms of ocean waves coming into shore. How often waves hit the shore is their frequency.

The wavelength refers to the distance between wave crests.

In light, wavelength multiplied by frequency equal a constant number—the speed of light. So as frequency gets higher, the wavelength shortens.

Infrared rays—what we recognize as heat—have a relatively long wavelength and slow frequency. Because these wavelengths in small doses can't hurt you, they are used in TV channel changers to switch stations.

Ultraviolet rays pulse at a faster frequency. Their shorter wavelengths penetrate your skin and burn you under your skin's surface.

X-rays have still higher frequencies and still shorter wavelengths. They go right through you.

The sun, with its huge energies, radiates all these frequencies and more.

A laser only radiates at one frequency band.

Because all its radiated energy is at one wavelength and it arrives in a single burst, it packs a powerful punch.

Instead of a bunch of wavelengths acting like people relaxing on a beach—some running, some walking, some lying down, some eating—all the energy in a laser beam marches ahead in step, like a military column. Its energy all hits at the same time. That's why it's powerful.

In a sense, laser light is like radio waves. Your radio can be tuned to pick up music or talk from a radio station because the information is being beamed at a specific frequency band. Laser beams are like that— they come at you at a particular frequency— only they're light waves instead of radio waves, and they don't have other information encoded in them.

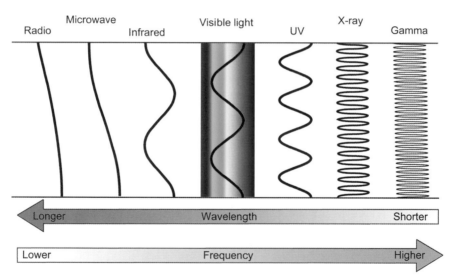

As the frequencies of light increase and the wavelength shortens, beams become more energetic. (Drawing by Xuan Chen)

Try this. You can see the difference between an ordinary flashlight and a pencil laser if you take both and shine them on a distant wall, say 20 feet (six meters) away. The laser beam will remain relatively strong and focused. Blam, its beam hits the wall and makes a small bright dot. It's bright and accurate enough that lecturers use laser "pointers" instead of the old-fashioned wooden dowels of days past. The flashlight beam, on the other hand, will spread out, become dim, and (yawn) barely make it across the room.

At NIF, all this light will flood a tiny capsule about two millimeters in size.

NIF's light stays at the same frequency until it reaches almost the very end of its journey. Then, to more deeply penetrate its target, it will pass through crystals that change the light to ultraviolet—the frequency component in sunshine that doesn't just feel hot on top of your skin but burns into layers of it.

The deeper penetration of ultraviolet light into the target is so important that NIF designers accepted a further loss in laser beam power. Earlier, we saw that the flashlamps were only 75 percent efficient in converting electrical energy to light. Then the neodymium took only 5 percent of that light. Now, by passing the infrared beam through several crystals to shorten its wavelength from infrared (at a wavelength of 1,053 nanometers) to ultraviolet (at a wavelength of 351 nanometers), the beam loses more than half its remaining power.

Specifically, the beam's power drops from 4.2 million joules to 1.8 million joules, emerging at 43 percent of its incoming power.

In terms of overall efficiency, the total ratio of NIF's radiated output power to electric input power is currently about 0.5 percent. To achieve a positive power result, from wall current to final output, the percentage must be raised.

Yet the output should still be strong enough to compress the target capsule to 20 times the density of lead.

But will this mighty pulse be useful as an energy source? Will it power an electrical generator for humanity?

How big is two millimeters in inches? A millimeter is a tenth of a centimeter. That sounds pretty small. How small? Find out by dividing 1 (inch) by 2.5 (the number of centimeters in one inch). I got that a centimeter is about 40 percent of an inch; what did you get? So a millimeter—one-tenth of a centimeter—is 4 percent of an inch. Two millimeters is 8 percent of an inch. The size of the NIF target, focus of the most powerful lasers on earth, of a machine that takes up three football fields, is just under a tenth of an inch.

And then to create fusion, the target has to shrink at about one-tenth the speed of light to become one-thirtieth its original size and 20 times the density of lead—an element already very dense.

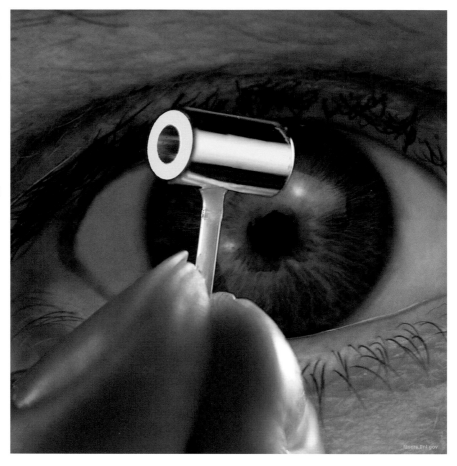

A NIF hohlraum, posed next to a human eye for scale. The cylinder is intended to hold a fusion capsule within it. The capsule is about the size of a small pea. (Courtesy Lawrence Livermore National Laboratory and National Security, LLC, and the US Department of Energy)

In *Star Trek* terms, will it support warp drive to power the *Enterprise*?

To make it so, NIF scientists will have to develop a method that fires its lasers several times a minute. This would be enough to drive a generator that can produce a continuous amount of electricity.

Originally, like Z, NIF was meant to produce the conditions of fusion only for further study of nuclear weapons and of stars. Its mighty lasers were expected to fire every few hours to let its neodymium-doped glass cool down. The lasers also had to be kept rigorously clean, in "clean rooms" a million times cleaner than ordinary air, because even the smallest particle of dust on one of the lasers could absorb enough heat to cause a temperature imbalance that might explode the glass of its optics.

So NIF has the same problem in becoming an energy generator as that faced by Z: NIF can fire a mighty pulse of light, but the next pulse by present means will take too long to fire to produce a workable electrical generator.

And while the machine's overall power is very high, delivered in nanoseconds into a tiny area, its overall energy generated—remember the difference between energy and power?—may not be large enough to create enough fusion to run a power plant.

But new thoughts are in the air. It's possible that tubes filled with cooled helium (as ITER will do) might be placed alongside the laser tubes to keep them cool when firing. Cool-down time then would be shortened, so rapidity of firing could increase.

Also, conventional glass could be replaced with ceramics or crystal—much hardier materials, cutting potential downtime because of scoring or breakage from heat or physical accidents.

Flashlamps could be out. Although they are impressive technology, they really seem to belong in 1940s black-and-white movies, in the era of news photographers with flashbulb cameras. Instead, solid-state diode light sources could be useful. The efficiencies of diodes in energizing neodymium could be as high as 60 to 80 percent because diodes can be fabricated to put out only the desired frequency instead of the mostly wasted energy range of white light. They could also fire rapidly, offering steady pulses of energy to energize NIF's main laser beam.

Unfortunately, today's diodes cannot generate the power needed to generate laser beams powerful enough to fuse isotopes.

But the future . . . That's where you come in . . .

CHAPTER 7
Fusion Confusion

If you could afford an airplane trip to, say, San Francisco or New York, usually you'll be there in a few hours. The technology works.

If you had a tooth cavity, presumably you'd go to a dentist.

But when the usual technologies fail, delay, or just plain don't excite us, adventurous people may turn to less proven solutions.

Some people have spent years concentrating on a yogic technique that promises a soul can leave its body and fly wherever it wants to go—say, San Francisco or New York—on minitrips. This technology is unproven.

I had an uncle who loved his wife so much that when she contracted an incurable cancer and they had exhausted every conventional means of treatment, he fed her shark cartilage because sharks were not known to get cancer. Maybe there was a cancer-fighting agent in the cartilage. Medical people shook their head, but my aunt lived three years beyond her prognosis before the cancer took its toll. Was my uncle right or was he wrong?

In the same spirit, some people tire of what seems an endless and expensive search for practical nuclear fusion.

They're sitting in the backseat of a car on a trip that seems to be taking forever. Every time they call, "Are we there yet?" the answer comes back from fusion scientists in the driver's seat, "Not yet."

So it's not surprising that some of the backseat passengers try less orthodox means. Maybe there's a better way.

Cold Fusion

Perhaps you'd like fusion in a jar? Maybe we don't need to spend billions of dollars, use up the working lives of hundreds of scientists, and build huge fusion plants 10 stories high or the lengths of several football fields.

Maybe we can make a little bit of fusion in the equivalent of a peanut butter jar. Then we could put the jar in our bathrooms or garages. Every household with its own little fusion generator to power lights, sound system, refrigerator, washing machine, and air conditioning. No more bills from the power company. No more area-wide electrical blackouts. It's an attractive concept.

Diagram for "cold fusion" apparatus: the little device that almost changed the world, except that its results never proved it could fuse atoms and release nuclear energy. (Drawing by Xuan Chen)

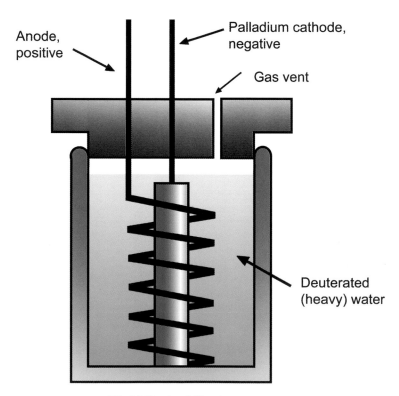

Anode, positive

Palladium cathode, negative

Gas vent

Deuterated (heavy) water

"Cold Fusion" Device

Two scientists proposed essentially this idea in 1989. They got a lot of publicity. Even though they were in Utah—not exactly a media hot spot—when they called a press conference to announce what they believed they could do, many media folk came. Because controlled nuclear fusion is very important. If these two scientists—Stanley Pons and Martin Fleischmann—could do what they said, it was big news.

Here's how they thought they had done it.

They modified a technique called electrolysis.

Electrolysis involves the passage of an electric current through an electrolyte—a liquid that's usually chiefly water. Two metal posts are placed in the electrolyte and hooked up by wires to an electrical charger. Current from the charger passes through the posts, creating an electric current traveling through the water. The charge breaks water molecules, H_2O, into ions, with hydrogen ions going to the cathode. There they pick up electrons re-entering the solution, become whole atoms, and emerge into the air as hydrogen gas.

Pons and Fleischmann modified this procedure.

Their posts, instead of being made of ordinary material like iron (as in a car battery), were made of a metal called palladium.

Instead of ordinary water, the researchers' test cells contained so-called heavy water, in which deuterium is substituted for ordinary hydrogen.

They passed a current through those posts into this solution.

Palladium behaves differently from iron. It doesn't release deuterium from water as an airborne gas. That's important because deuterium fleeing into the atmosphere would be useless in creating fusion. Instead, palladium's lattice structure stores these atoms like tenants in an apartment building. The deuterium isotope, with its extra neutron, is stored no differently from ordinary hydrogen as it diffuses through palladium's lattice structure.

It's stored very close together with other deuterium atoms.

You recall that the trick of fusion is to bring atoms like deuterium close enough together, in high enough concentrations, that they can fuse.

So, how close together can the palladium lattice store deuterium atoms?

Not close enough.

But certainly the reaction seemed to be generating heat. Something was happening.

If the deuterium atoms somehow interacted with and cracked the palladium structure, allowing the deuterium nuclei to come still closer together, somehow generating an additional electric current with a strong, accompanying magnetic field for compression, they might be brought close enough together to fuse.

According to Fleischmann and Pons, this was the case.

The generated heat, as well as neutrons that their instruments showed had been emitted, seemed to prove their container contained an ongoing fusion reaction.

Naturally, there was a worldwide furor over this.

Some scientists said, That's all it took? You put two sticks of metal in a solution of heavy water and the atoms fuse and we get energy? We've been wasting 50 years, whole working lifetimes, on these complex and expensive and time-consuming experiments and two dudes in Utah solved the problem in the equivalent of a peanut butter jar?

It didn't help the credibility of what came to be called *cold fusion* that the information on its success had been released at a press conference. Usually, new results are published first in scientific journals, where they are pre-reviewed for credibility and accuracy by other scientists.

Furthermore, Pons and Fleischmann had released few details of their method because they intended to patent the process.

Naturally, there were accusations and counteraccusations. Most old-line scientists tried to achieve the same results but couldn't and came very close to calling the newly proposed method fraudulent.

They said, "If this is really a fusion reaction, it would release high-energy neutrons, which are deadly. So why aren't the researchers dead?"

At the same time, researchers who had duplicated the experiments as best they could believed they had seen some neutrons, or a rise in temperature corresponding to an increased output of energy. They felt that the old guard was just defending an expensive and outmoded way of doing things.

Because it's science, the controversy went on for years. There's no single authority to decree, Stop the controversy. There's no one leader. Everyone's got a say. No one's got the answer. Some scientists believed and did more experiments to prove their belief. Others worked to prove the opposite.

Most scientists, after a while, stopped trying to prove it one way or the other because there were few institutions willing to pay for their experiments. The gloss had worn off the idea, and it was clear there would be no immediate results in producing electricity. Many researchers found the ongoing controversy an embarrassment to science. Yet certain scientists of some note thought there was something curious happening in the reaction but were afraid to publicly come out and say so. These scientists were afraid to be derided by their peers and suffer damage to their reputations.

Imagine that everyone in your group seems to believe some particular thing, but you believe they are wrong. For example, they believe the earth is flat and the sun goes around it. You believe the earth is round and travels around the sun. You could tell them they're wrong, but how would you get them to listen? Would you just state your opinion? Would you try to prove your opinion? How far would you be willing to go before you backed down because the group said you were stupid or obnoxious (even if you were right)? (And what if, on a different issue, you were wrong?)

Over time, evidence seemed to be accumulating that no fusion reaction was taking place in the jar, although a chemical reaction might be.

But some people still believe in the cold fusion process. They give presentations on their research at physics conferences. These researchers are rarer as time passes. Still, it's science. No one knows for sure.

Other short, simple methods of achieving fusion have met difficulties when further tests by scientists were applied.

Sonofusion

In 2002, so-called bubble fusion, or sonofusion—the attempt to achieve fusion through sound waves—was reported. The original term for this work is *sonoluminescence*—to create light using sound.

The idea was to heat acetone, the active ingredient in nail polish remover and paint thinners and plastics. The acetone had been "deuterated"—that is, deuterium had been joined to it. Researchers led by Rusi Taleyarkhan at Purdue University sent a beam of neutrons into the mix as "seeds" for bubbles. Then a sound wave sent vibrations into the mixture. Sonic waves caused bubbles to form, expand, and then suddenly collapse. This was thought to bring their components—among them, deuterium and neutrons—suddenly and intensely together. The reaction caused flashes of light that led to the method being called a "star in a jar."

According to Taleyarkhan's team, the collapse was so sudden and so hot that fusion occurred between deuterium atoms. Fusion neutrons were emitted and tritium was found, according to his team's instruments, indicating the joining of neutrons and deuterium.

Cheap, simple, easy.

Other researchers couldn't verify the results.

So the Taleyarkhan team tried again, using tougher criteria.

Other researchers tried to simplify the experiment by not using neutrons to seed bubbles; then if free neutrons were found above the normal background levels, they would have to be caused by a fusion reaction.

To date, this method—like cold fusion—has not proven out.

Tabletop Fusion

But not all is hopeless for brief methods. Tabletop fusion has indeed been achieved in at least two locations. It was reported at Lawrence Livermore National Laboratory in 1999 and again at the University of California at Los Angeles (UCLA) in 2005.

At Lawrence Livermore, instead of the customary gigantic facilities, fusion was reportedly taking place on a lab bench about three feet (one meter) wide and 10 feet (three meters) long.

Todd Ditmire and colleagues focused a powerful laser briefly on a small volume of deuterium. The superheated ions became an exploding plasma that smashed deuterium ions into each other, releasing fusion neutrons.

So, game over? We can go home now? The home team has solved the fusion energy problem?

Not exactly. The method requires about 10 million times more laser energy than can be harvested from the reaction, which occurs too quickly to produce usable energy. (A fusion reaction of this type must last, as it does for Z and will for NIF, at least a few nanoseconds. Ditmire's lasted about 0.2 nanosecond.)

Reproducibility of results is a cornerstone of science. It's not enough to claim to have witnessed or produced a remarkable thing. Other scientists must be able to follow the same procedures and come up with the same result. Otherwise, something could be wrong with the first scientist's equipment. Or maybe the first team is just seeing what it wants to see. Or there might even be fraud.

In this approach, science is unique.

When the Bible says that the people of Israel, leaving Egypt, followed a cloud by day and a pillar of fire by night, it's dramatic. You believe it or you don't. But you can't prove or disprove it.

For a song to be successful, it must hit something in the emotions of the listener in different cities or even countries. But no one knows how to bottle that appeal and reproduce it in song after song. The key ingredient isn't easily replicated.

In science, claims have to be demonstrated by reproducible results. This means that other scientists, following the procedures the first scientist laid out, should come up with the same results. An apple falling from a tree should take the same time to hit the ground in Hawaii as New York or Italy, assuming the tree branch is the same height and other atmospheric and gravitational factors are the same.

If a scientist's results can survive the acid tests of many people trying to duplicate them, maybe a scientific advance has been made.

It could serve as a compact source of neutrons for studying material. And it was a remarkable achievement.

Researchers Seth Putterman, Brian Naranjo, and Jim Gimzewski at UCLA had a different idea. They put deuterium gas around a crystal. A tiny tungsten pin, impregnated with deuterium, was inserted in the crystal so it stuck out like a lighthouse.

Heating the crystal produced an electric field and its accompanying magnetic field. The gas started swirling, got ionized, and crashed into the pin.

Deuterium fused.

Fusion neutrons were released.

The problem? The reaction produces so few neutrons, compared to the energy put in to make them, that the method could never be an energy-producing machine. It's a good source of neutrons for scientific study, though, and could have further applications in medicine and space.

Meson Fusion

I've saved the most complicated for last.

Cosmic rays contain an atomic particle called a muon that can have negative charge, like an electron, but is 207 times heavier. That means if a muon is substituted for an electron, a muonic hydrogen atom is only 1/207 the size of a normal hydrogen atom. (The radius of the orbit is inversely proportional to its mass.)

So, what have we here? A muonic hydrogen atom much smaller than a normal hydrogen atom. The muon, by shielding the hydrogen nucleus's positive charge, can bring its nucleus much closer to the nuclei of other atoms, making fusion more likely.

Scientists have worked with muons since their discovery in 1947 by Charles Frank at Bristol University in England.

The problem with muonic fusion is that, first of all, the life of a muon is very brief—about 2.2 millionths of a second. Second, to produce muons in an accelerator takes about 1,000 times more energy than is released by a single deuterium-tritium interaction. (An accelerator is a machine that can create new atomic particles by smashing known ones together at high speeds.)

Still, it seemed possible that a muon could be released after a muonic DT interaction and very quickly join up with another deuterium, catalyzing that reaction. And then another. And then another, like a quick-draw cowboy firing shot after shot. (A catalyst helps a desired reaction to occur faster, while remaining unchanged itself. Thus, at no cost, like volunteer labor, it helps do the same work over and over.)

However, to be cost-effective, a muon would have to catalyze 1,000 deuterium-tritium interactions in its short life.

Calculations by the famous Russian physicist Andrei Sakharov seemed to show the process would be too slow to produce a net gain in energy.

Equally famous physicist Luis Alvarez at the University of California at Berkeley in 1956 observed muonic fusion actually occurring.

Work led by Stephen Jones at Los Alamos National Laboratory in 1985 showed that under pressure, approximately 150 fusions per muon could be achieved in the particle's short life span.

This was still not enough to make it effective as an energy source.

But work continues on muon-catalyzed fusion in projects in several countries.

Maybe you can be the one who finds a shortcut to fusion.

You would be remembered forever.

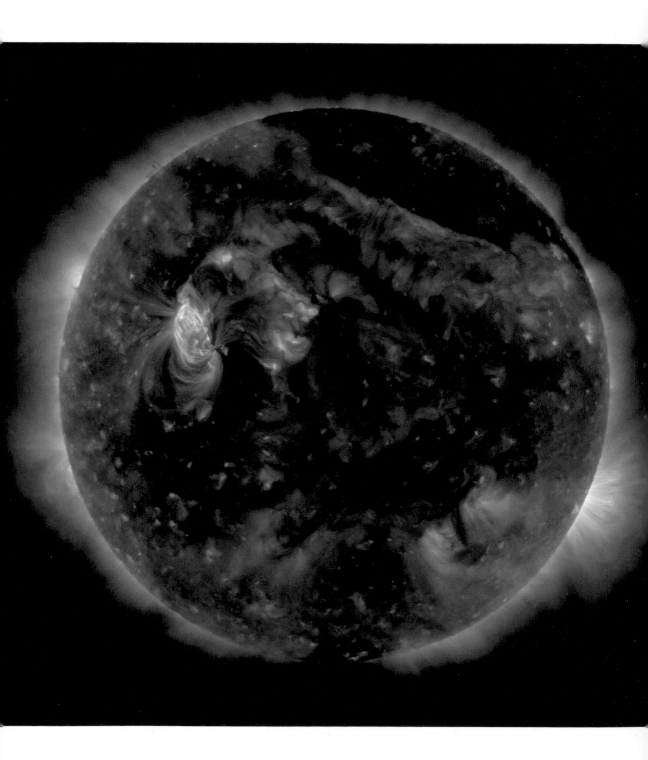

CHAPTER 8

Fusion Conclusion

Everything Changes

The world as you grow up can seem made of stone. Parents, teachers, classes, homework.

Actually, it's written in water. Everything is flexible. I'm not talking about moral standards, which are beyond the scope of this book. I mean scientifically.

Four hundred years ago, people believed the sun went around the earth. Wrong.

A hundred years ago, there were riots in Washington, DC, over the idea that there were multiple galaxies in the universe. Now it's commonly accepted.

So it's not surprising, looking at fusion, that though these machines as I've reported them are big and expensive and very much *there*, you can expect all sorts of changes. Z, an electrically powered machine, 15 years ago was shooting beams of lithium ions at targets. Now it uses a kind of natural, homegrown magnetic field created by its own electricity to control its plasma. But it's already borrowing a laser from NIF to use as a camera. Then the laser may be used to preheat a fusion capsule, borrowing again from NIF. Who's to say what else Z may borrow or invent by the time you become a scientist? Will a spherical target still be used? Will it borrow from ITER and bring in, somehow, more intentional magnetism to implode a pellet faster or more controllably? Even the golden hohlraum, once thought essential in creating an oven to cook the fusion capsule, is no longer as prominent. Instead, something called a dynamic hohlraum is in use, where the wire ions, imploding, send a shock wave into an intermediate wall of foam, squeezing and heating it to high temperatures so that it becomes its own hohlraum, no gold needed. The foam, as it becomes smaller (a process called dynamic compression), transmits x-rays into the fusion capsule at its center. X-rays must travel inward because they are blocked by the ions collapsing behind them from traveling outward.

No one knows what tomorrow will bring. You could make that new tomorrow happen.

NIF has huge lasers—but they don't fire fast. One day those lasers may be replaced by rapidly firing diodes, if they ever become

This deceptively simple diagram of the dynamic hohlraum uses low-density plastic foam instead of a gold container to hold the fusion capsule. (Courtesy Sandia National Laboratories)

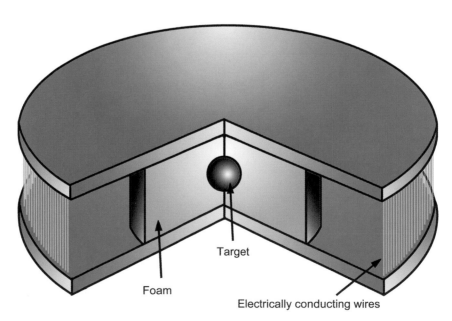

Target

Foam

Electrically conducting wires

powerful enough. Who knows what the project will require then? More electricity? More magnetism? Will it become more efficient? Could these lasers metamorphose into the fusion machine of the future? No one knows.

The ITER donut is a convincing way to hold plasma at more than a hundred million degrees. The machine keeps ions encircled by magnetic fields and always moving forward through the donut so they never have time to think or get their bearings—move along there, little ions. But maybe the donut will be replaced by a sphere. There's some evidence that plasma may be more stable traversing that shape. Maybe the shape of the donut itself will change. Maybe it will become a pretzel; who knows?

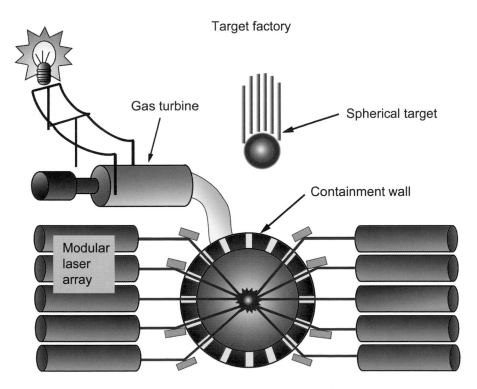

The HAPL (High Average Power Laser) program at the Naval Research Laboratory shines an array of powerful lasers onto a frozen target dropped into the firing chamber of the machine. The target, compressed, releases neutrons that are then captured by the chamber wall and their energy converted into electricity. One of the simpler major efforts. (Drawing by Xuan Chen)

Machines we haven't discussed here may come to the fore. The Naval Research Laboratory's High Average Power Laser (HAPL) program may prove successful.

An under-construction laser project called the *Laser Megajoule Facility* (LMJ) that resembles NIF is under construction in southern France. It will come online later than NIF, but its researchers may learn from NIF's experiences to improve their own machine.

A possible proton-boron fusion reaction being studied doesn't even involve radioactivity—that is, no neutrons would be released should fusion be achieved. Right now, such a reaction takes an unrealistic amount of heat to occur, reportedly far above the 100 million degrees of ITER and NIF. Perhaps, though, new knowledge will make this reaction a possibility for useful fusion.

Other methods claim to function without the need for magnetic fields.

No one knows what changes will come.

But they *will* come because the subject is so important and its possible benefits so immense. As the earth's population expands and its natural resources and open space simultaneously diminish, one of the most critical questions for the human race will be its energy source.

And there it is, waiting for us, however we can make it happen: nuclear fusion, the natural phenomenon we see sailing above our heads almost every day as the sun.

Filled with so much energy we can hardly look at it.

Waiting for you to discover how to create and harness it here on earth.

If You Want to Know More about Nuclear Fusion . . .

The pace of future explorations of nuclear fusion is unpredictable. The following are some additional sources that help explain what fusion is, how far research has come, and ways to stay up-to-date with fusion progress as time passes.

The Net is an easy resource, of course, but it comes with two major problems. One, Net sites wink on and wink out, so something recommended by me today may not be there when you key in its address. Two, material on the Net is unvetted—that is, anyone can say anything and if they link it to the term *nuclear fusion*, there it is. You can waste a lot of time reading, and being thrilled or bored by, theories not backed up by hard-nosed experiments, competent computer simulations, or classical mathematics. Nevertheless, here are some sites (and books) that should work.

Websites

www.iter.org

The ITER website is wonderfully dense and has kept up reasonably well with current work. It has photos and artists' conceptions of the work and links to links that link to links to take you in, or as far back, as you probably care to go. In addition to simple explanations, it carries technical papers and even job openings.

http://lasers.llnl.gov/

The NIF website is similarly detailed and worth examining for the latest news and history of that impressive laser-driven effort. It may not detail technical problems but will certainly explain successes and dreams. This site may become particularly important when the first NIF fusion shot takes place.

http://zpinch.sandia.gov/

The Z website is slender but improving. If you go there, you will see the cool picture of Z firing (also on the cover of this book). You may also see the cool, little-known Z logo—a blue Z hanging in space like a spaceship's track, its sharpened bottom line heading like a spear (or the spaceship *Enterprise* in overdrive) into the heart of what could be a blazing yellow sun or distant solar system. Descriptions, images, and videos are less exuberant than on ITER or NIF sites, but cover the ground in a kind of engineer's view. The Wikipedia Z-machine entry gives a short, somewhat technical overview of the machine. Also, Googling *z machine at sandia labs* calls up links to news releases and articles written about the machine. If these pieces come directly from Sandia National Laboratories, they are at least vetted by scientists and are probably correct. (I wrote most of them.) Other articles that appeared in reputable magazines are also probably worth a look.

Books

How Things Work—The Physics of Everyday Life,
by Louis A. Bloomfield (Wiley, 1997)
A brief, simple, well-written description of efforts in nuclear fusion can be found in chapter 18 of this book. The chapter starts very properly with nuclear fission reactors (since they exist), mentions their dangers, and moves into nuclear fusion. The chapter's epilogue

(along with other books) mentions the difficulty humans faced pre-20th century in understanding why the sun burns.

Fusion: The Energy of the Universe,
by Garry McCracken and Peter Stott (Elsevier, 2005)
The Fusion Quest, by T. Kenneth Fowler
(Johns Hopkins University Press, 1997)
Excellent but college-level explanations of nuclear fusion efforts can be found in these two books, written by physicists and full of useful information. The Fowler book is currently out of print, but libraries have it.

Physics for Future Presidents, by Richard A. Muller (Norton, 2008)
Physics of the Impossible, by Michio Kaku (Doubleday, 2008)
Brief, well-written fusion discussions for the general public are included in these popular books that scan a range of science. Both books describe roadblocks in attaining high-yield fusion but are hopeful of its eventual achievement.

An Elementary Treatise on Electricity,
by James Clerk Maxwell (2nd edition, Dover, 2005)
All the work described in this book came about over the last two centuries as scientists began probing the nature of electricity and magnetism. If you read the reports of researchers of the 19th century, you can feel how tentative they were with these new forces. It was a bit like finding a new animal—they had no idea of what it could do or why it existed. An inexpensive way to feel the thrill of that blind time is to read snippets from Maxwell's book. Maxwell, one of the earliest explorers of this invisible world, was an English scientist who lived in the middle of the 19th century. Read the exact way he describes what we now take for granted, carefully creating a map of the steps of his

experiments. You can feel the mystery of the uncharted territories through which he trod. Einstein later characterized Maxwell's work as "the most profound and the most fruitful that physics has experienced since the time of Newton."

Glossary

alpha particle: The same as a helium nucleus. It's created in fusion reactions and has a positive charge and a little less mass than the four hydrogen atoms that can form it. That missing mass, in the sun and in experiments on earth, became energy.

ampere: A unit of electric current.

atom: The smallest unit of matter known in which an element keeps its chemical properties. Break up an atom and its parts no longer resemble that element.

blanket: In a fusion context, it's a lithium-based wall that interacts with free neutrons to form tritium used to continue the fusion reaction.

breeder reaction: In fusion, where tritium can be made, or "bred," from the interaction of neutrons with a lithium blanket surrounding the fusion plasma.

capacitor: A device made of two metal plates that stores electric charge. An insulating layer separates the plates.

cold fusion: The apparently failed attempt to create controlled nuclear fusion by causing isotopes of hydrogen to stack in the crystalline structure of a palladium rod. Think of the rod as a kind of apartment house where the "rooms" stack heavy hydrogen more closely together than they normally would be found if they were, say, picnicking together in an open field. Because the stacking overcomes the natural distance hydrogen atoms keep from each other, the researchers believed that under certain circumstances their nuclei might begin to fuse, giving up neutrons, a sign of atomic fusion.

deformable mirror: A mirror built of adjustable sub-mirrors. The angle of the sub-mirrors can be varied to correct distortions in images.

deuterium: A hydrogen atom with a neutron added to its nucleus.

divertor: In ITER, a location where the machine's magnetic field is modified to divert unwanted particles from the plasma reaction area into another region of the machine.

doped: Deliberately contaminating a substance with an impurity that changes its properties.

electron: Part of an atom, an electron has a single negative charge and is much smaller than a proton. Originally, it was thought that an electron resembles a planet circling the sun in terms of its size and distance from the atom's nucleus. Later theories are more complicated.

element: Atoms with unique numbers of protons in their nuclei, giving each element its distinctive properties.

energy: The capacity to do work. Less formally, it's the capacity to make things happen.

frequency: How fast something occurs. With wavelengths, it's the amount of time it takes for a wave to oscillate one complete cycle.

fusion capsule: A small spherical packet that may contain deuterium and tritium enclosed in a thin shell. Z, NIF and other pulsed-power efforts may use capsules as targets for x-rays that can produce fusion. Z has already succeeded; NIF may do so.

gauss: A unit of magnetic field strength.

gravity: The attractive force between masses. The reason we don't fly off into space as the earth turns. The reason apples fall to the ground. Why the earth circles the sun instead of flying off into interstellar space.

heavy water: Ordinary water is made of hydrogen and oxygen. Heavy water is made up of hydrogen isotope deuterium and water. Deuterium has an extra neutron in its nuclei, making its mass about twice as big as that of a normal hydrogen atom. Thus, it's "heavier." Thus, heavy water.

helium: An element consisting of two protons, two neutrons, and two electrons.

high-yield fusion: A fusion reaction that produces more energy than used to create the reaction.

hohlraum: A tiny oven used in some forms of pulsed power to hold the fusion capsule. Usually of gold, the walls reflect x-rays from every angle into the capsule, causing its outer layers to burn off and its inner layers to contract evenly—the same amount at every point. Think of it as an oven helping to evenly cook a turkey.

hydrogen: The lightest element. It consists of one proton and one electron. Isotopes of hydrogen are deuterium and tritium. These also have one proton and one electron but contain one and two neutrons, respectively, in the nuclei.

ignition: When things start to burn; in fusion, when the capsule's contents begin to fuse on their own like a piece of paper taking fire.

inertial confinement fusion: The attempt to use a pulse of energy, whether electrical or light, to compress a spherical capsule so suddenly that component atoms fuse, producing neutrons.

instabilities: The undesirable distortions of magnetic fields over time in the attempts to contain both pulsed power fusion and magnetic confinement fusion.

ion: An atom with either more or fewer electrons than the stable atomic version. Ions can be influenced by magnetic fields.

isotope: A variation of an atom. The atom and its isotope are the same except that an isotope has more neutrons in its nuclei. Deuterium and tritium are isotopes of hydrogen.

ITER: The largest experimental magnetic fusion project in the world, in Cadarache, France. ITER in Latin means "the way." The former meaning of the acronym was "international thermonuclear experimental reactor." The machine will attempt to contain, using magnetic fields, a plasma hotter than the sun.

Kurchatov Institute: Russia's leading institute for fusion research, where the first successful magnetic confinement was briefly achieved in a machine called a tokomak.

laser: An acronym that stands for light amplified by the stimulated emission of radiation. Lasers send out light of a single frequency, called monochromatic. Because the laser light's wavelengths are, so to speak, in step, they have a coherence and power that ordinary light lacks.

Laser Megajoule Facility (LMJ): A more powerful version of the NIF. Under construction in southern France, the LMJ is expected to be completed later than the NIF.

magnetic confinement fusion: The attempt to confine a burning plasma, heated hotter than the sun, with magnetic fields produced by ultracold magnets.

mass: The property of an object that causes it to have weight in a gravitational field and to resist change in its motion.

molecule: Joined atoms; can be more than two.

neodymium: An element used to dope the glass of the NIF lasers.

neutron: A combination of an electron and a proton. It's called a neutron because it's electrically neutral: the positive charge on the proton and the negative electron cancel each other out, like a married couple where one votes Democrat and the other Republican.

National Ignition Facility (NIF): The National Ignition Facility at Lawrence Livermore National Laboratory in Livermore,

California, expects to focus a powerful pulse of light from 192 lasers onto a tiny capsule to create a burst of fusion.

nuclear fission: The splitting (fissioning) of large atoms to produce energy.

nuclear fusion: The joining of two light atoms to form a heavier one, releasing energy in the process.

nucleus: The center of an atom.

parameter: A distinguishing characteristic or feature.

pinch effect: The compression of a cloud of ions by a magnetic field generated by an electric current.

plasma: A mob of electrons and ions in the form of a hot gas. Plasma is sometimes referred to as the fourth state of matter, after liquid, solid, and gas. It is the state of matter most often found in the universe.

polarize: To cause light waves to vibrate in a particular orientation.

proton: A particle found in the nuclei of atoms. It has a single positive charge.

pulsed power: Energy compressed in time to achieve a more powerful effect. You could slowly gather water behind a dam for weeks, but if you release that water in a few minutes, you get a powerful force. It's the same amount of water but released in a much shorter time than it was accumulated. Similarly, electricity accumulated slowly can produce an overwhelming effect if released suddenly.

radioactive: Spontaneous decomposition of the nuclei of atoms.

short circuit: A usually accidental, low-resistance bridge between two electricity-carrying wires.

sonoluminescence: Bubbles in a liquid created by sound waves (sono-). The bubbles release light, becoming luminescent.

superconductors: Materials that at low temperatures lose their resistance to the passage of electricity. Such materials can create very strong magnetic fields.

supernova: The explosion of a star, which becomes extremely bright for a short time and emits vast amounts of energy. In this furnace, the higher (more complicated) elements are thought to be forged.

tokomak: The magnetic confinement system to be used by ITER in its attempts to control plasma as nuclei fuse. It was first proposed in 1951 by two Russian scientists, Andrei Sakharov and Igor Tamm. The word is an acronym from the Russian words TOroidalnaya KAmera ee MAgnitaya Katushka, or "Toroidal Chamber with Magnetic Coil."

torus: A donut-shaped containment vessel.

tritium: A radioactive isotope of hydrogen with two neutrons in its nuclei. It has a half-life of about 12 years.

turbulence: When liquids or gases swirl erratically and, in many cases, unpredictably.

volt: If amperes are fish swimming in a river, volts are the height of the waterfall down which they must fall to reach your appliances. They can be thought of as potential energy. A US household electric line is approximately 120 volts.

wavelength: The distance a wave travels to make a complete oscillation.

wire array: At Sandia National Laboratories Z machine, a group of very thin wires through which huge electric currents are passed.

Z machine: A pulsed power machine at Sandia National Laboratories in Albuquerque, New Mexico, that uses powerful bursts of electricity to compress fusion targets.

Illustration Credits

Welcome to
Worlds of Wonder

A Young Reader's Science Series

Advisory Editors: David Holtby and Karen Taschek

In these engagingly written and beautifully illustrated books, the University of New Mexico Press seeks to convey to young readers the thrill of science as well as to inspire further inquiry into the wonders of scientific research and discovery.

ALSO AVAILABLE IN THE BARBARA GUTH WORLDS OF WONDER SERIES:

Hanging with Bats: Ecobats, Vampires, and Movie Stars
by Karen Taschek

The Tree Rings' Tale: Understanding Our Changing Climate
by John Fleck

What Are Global Warming and Climate Change? by Chuck McCutcheon

Powering the Future: New Energy Technologies by Eva Thaddeus

Eco-Tracking: On the Trail of Habitat Change by Daniel Shaw

Cell Phone Science: What Happens When You Call and Why
by Michele Sequiera and Michael Westphal

Index

Page numbers in *italics* indicate illustrations.

Yonas, Gerry, 36

zero, absolute, 45, 48
Z machine
    amps used by, 15, 16–17, 25–26,
      38, 40
    capabilities of, 22–23
    detail of, *14, 15, 16, 17, 35, 39, 40,
      41*
    evolution of, 31–42, 97–98
    funding, 67
    heat capacity of, 43

    high-yield hydrogen fusion as
      goal of, 23–29, 38
    inertial confinement fusion
    method used by, 20–21, 29, 41,
      56, 75
    magnetic strength of ITER
      machine v., 51
    plasma and, 18, 19, 26–27
    website, 102
    wire innovation with, 33–37
    Z pinch action of, 18, *19*, 20